You Too! Repeat "I deserve to Succeed!"

Lessons for Financial Success in 12 Easy to Follow Lessons

Jorge Ramirez

DEDICATION

We dedicate this work to all those who want to improve themselves and take an independent path with their own lives.

CONTENTS

ACKNOWLEDGMENTS

We would like to thank all those who made this possible – J.Norwood for his incredible research and observational acumen, my family, the publishers, and of course the readers who went over the manuscript to ensure it was helpful in the educational knowledge it provides. Thank you all for the incredible work done and provided, it is that creativity, tenacity, and dedication to improving the lives of all, which means so much.

1

PREFACE

A title for this work was difficult to come up with, since the authors desired to convey the content without sounding just like one of the other self-help books out there for the reading public. So it was decided to go with the bold and boisterous, after all go boldly!

Why did they want it to sound different? Well, that is simple to answer - the lessons herein are different. Before these words were put down for you the reader, the authors "walked the walk" and "talked the talk", they each individually applied these ideas in their own careers and business lives (over several decades) - to see how they worked and to show that they did indeed work. What you see here are the words being put down **AFTER** the testing has been completed.

Sadly, the world is full of self-help offerings in the form of seminars and other delivery mediums (DVDs, videos, pamphlets, to name a few) where the creator has not applied what they teach – you the reader of their works become the testers to prove the theory or not. If something is shown not to work, it is then corrected in a later volume and/or edition. As parting thought – think of the several publicized scandals in the self-help industry in the last 15 years.

This instructional book is a serious attempt to present the reader with information that can cause them to succeed in business once they have mastered the principles set forth herein and then applied these methods — recommended to them — to their own business and personal lives.

A work of this sort seems to be needed by the business world at this time, more than it has ever been needed before. "Capitalist mentality" and "Labor minded thoughts" apparently had come to regard themselves as eternal duelists engaged in a death struggle. The young person entering upon a business career, and observing this deadly conflict between these two classes of thought, naturally begins their careers with the impression that unless one is aligned only with a "Capitalist mentality" or with "Labor minded thoughts," success is impossible.

This is all wrong!

Why it is wrong, is made clear in the second lesson, on "Attitude."

Business is an "Exchange of Service(s)."

"Capitalist mentality" and "Labor minded thought" are but expressions of the same business principle — Service. Both are concerned with "Business." The operations of both require business ability and business people. There is but one law for both — the law of Service.

There are numerous works out there on "Applied Psychology" and "How to Succeed", works that have been written by persons who seem to experience great difficulty in convincing their readers there are really Natural laws governing success in business, quite as definite and infallible as other Natural laws, such as those governing the effect of gravity on falling bodies or capillary attraction as seen in a drinking straw.

These writers have been philosophers rather than business people. Their works are more alluring to the mystic, the dreamer, the altruist, than to the practical business person. One is constantly wondering whether the "rules," they enunciate have ever been really tested — especially by the writers.

Again, to reiterate, everything in this work has been put to the test by career business people. The authors themselves have demonstrated the principles they recommend to others. The "rules" always "work." And they "work" equally as well for an unskilled day laborer as for a bank president.

Yet the authors are keenly conscious of one great defect in this presentation of this theme, and that is, that in denying the natural and fundamental principles of business success, the precise meaning of the words used in the definition may elude many readers.

No way of overcoming this defect has been found by the authors because there seems to be absolutely no language of common usage, in which to define the abstruse terms used by scientists, philosophers and psychologists to explain the mental processes. This lack of a common terminology, while greatly to be deplored, necessitates the use of definitions in "plain English," upon which the greater number of the said scientists, philosophers and psychologists seem to be agreed.

However, not even this entirely eliminates the difficulty, because it sometimes happens that none of the individuals named are entirely clear in their own minds as to the precise meaning that should attach to their own expressions. They seem to be very much obtuse with their own explanations which do not explain. In such cases it has been customary to coin a word to cover up what they do not understand — and so it creeps into the dictionary to the eternal puzzlement of others. We can only try as best we may to further elucidate these coined words where their use seems forced upon us.

A notable instance of this is the word "Atom," once used to describe the smallest possible division of matter. Nowadays the "Atom" has become a world of "Electrons," each as relatively far from the center of the "Atom" as the earth is from the Sun!

What is of most importance in this book for business people, however, is that the exact meaning of the terms Consciousness, Self-Consciousness, and Sub-Consciousness be grasped by the reader. Especially is the word "Sub-Consciousness," as used in this work, susceptible to misinterpretation unless the entire text is carefully followed.

A NOTE ON "SUB-CONSCIOUSNESS"

The term is of such common usage among psychologists, that it was deemed unwise to abandon it in favor of a more precise yet unfamiliar name, since it has at least the virtue of conveying a more or less definite though inadequate idea, of what is meant.

But the terms "Sub-conscious" and "Sub-consciousness" do not express an exact, scientific psychology. While practical business people will be interested only in that degree of accuracy that will enable them to use their own mental powers intelligently, without bothering about the philosophical or scientific phases of the subject, yet it seems desirable at the outset to avoid more captious critics who may wish to argue the matter.

As pointed out by a friend whose knowledge of such matters far transcends that of the authors, the term "Latent Consciousness" would express the noun "Subconsciousness" much more scientifically. However, the word "latent" does not lend itself as an adjective, and its use might confuse rather than elucidate the subject — as to say, "latent-conscious mind," or "inactive" mind. There is **ONLY ONE MIND.**

Obviously the use of the term "Latent" instead of the prefix "Sub-" when speaking of that degree of Consciousness, would imply, what is strictly true, that the "contents" of consciousness are all there, but they are merely not active enough to reach the plane of our attention.

On the other hand, the meticulous stickler for common usage will see in the term "Sub," the indication that the content of consciousness is below the plane of consciousness; a manifest absurdity. What is meant by Sub-consciousness as herein used, is, of course, that the content is merely below the plane of attention — or not yet sufficiently active to intrude itself on attention.

With this note in mind, the reader should have no difficulty in comprehending other terms, which hinge upon this one.

The authors are greatly indebted to many friends who have lent assistance in editing this manuscript and suggesting its arrangement. Some very encouraging expressions of opinion have been given as to its value and possible popularity as a text book by those who not only want to know how to make their business efforts succeed, but who want to know the "why" of things.

Whatever will be its fate, it is now committed to the hands of those for whom it was written. All the authors can justly ask is, that they read carefully first, and then apply its principles, before proclaiming an opinion that it is "just one more inspirational book." For it is claimed for this work, that it presents an exact formula for success in business, based wholly upon Natural Law, and not at all depending for its "authority" upon human laws — which the great jurist, Sir William Blackstone, held, are attempts of humankind to pattern after the higher law, admitting that the patterns are all too frequently defective because of human ignorance of that higher law.

And, it is also claimed, that this work proclaims the Natural Law as the only sure method of success; that whatever measure of success any individual has or has ever had, must be due to their good fortune or their wisdom in aligning themselves with Natural Law.

--The Authors.

2

INTRODUCTION

SELF-CONTROL IS THE GREAT "SECRET OF SUCCESS."

Failures are never made by people possessed of the ability to control themselves, because Success is the natural consequence of working with Natural Law, and all Self-controlled individuals work with this law. To work with the law is the nature of Self-control.

But what is involved in the achievement of Self-control?

And how will a student who has never made a success of business, be so instructed in the infallible, Natural Laws that govern success, that they can apply the methods pointed out to them, to their own situation, with such intelligence that they will achieve results, regardless of their belief or disbelief in their efficacy?

Mere statements of fact, without full explanations of all details connected with the reasons for making the statements, will convey little information to the student who has not already made a success of business. If a mere formula would suffice, then the rules of success, in business or any other line of human endeavor, might be stated as follows, and this little work be brought to a close.

1. Be ambitious — **WANT SOMETHING**.

2. Have a definite purpose in wanting it.

3. Concentrate your whole attention on achieving your purpose.

4. Make your attitude toward your work, one of the pleasures. If your attitude is one of aversion and you cannot change it, then abandon your work for something to your liking.

5. Use your energy efficiently by working in silence, which stops up leaks and prevents waste of energy.

6. Increase your power by stimulating your emotions and bringing them under control. Any emotion is powerful and can be directed and utilized to perform work, if brought under self-control, by will.

7. Acquire Vision by use of imagination in building from memories evoked by emotion.

8. Take the initiative; mastery demands this.

Obviously, these eight simple directions need further elucidation for the student who is inexperienced in their practical application. Numerous questions will inevitably arise in their mind as to the exact meaning of such terms as the following:

- Attitude
- Attention
- Energy
- Silence
- Vision
- Emotion
- Memory
- Initiative
- Purpose
- Ambition
- Achievement
- Mastery

Under these twelve specific heads, therefore, I have attempted to point out the definite, straight road to business success, in twelve lessons that define the natural meaning of all the terms used. Referring to your dictionary will help. But dictionaries give commonly accepted usage of words as they appear in present-day language. The popular usage is not always the original meaning of the word.

No apology is offered for any lack of literary skill in presenting these lessons. Their object is not literary perfection, but to instruct those who want to know. Nor is any apology offered for failure to discuss certain fascinating problems arising out of allusions to scientific, mystical, philosophical and religious analogies by which I have endeavored to make the Natural Laws of Business clearer to the student.

Such discussions have no place in a volume devoted to teaching business people and women, and would-be business people and women, how to achieve success; or if they are already "successful," how to be more so.

Certain statements made in the lessons to follow, will doubtless meet with criticism, incredulity, even with ridicule. I do not defend the statements nor care to argue with the critics. All that I ask of anyone, is to submit the statements to a personal test before pronouncing them erroneous.

No plea is made that the reader do all or any of the things herein pointed out as the essentials of success. That is entirely the reader's affair. But the unqualified assertion is made, that everyone of ordinary intelligence, who does these things, will succeed in business under a Natural Law of Success that works as unceasingly and is as inevitable in its results as the Law of Gravity.

When I have myself used and demonstrated the value of the methods I now present to others, and when friends to whom I have given the same instruction, inform me of results attained, it is natural that I feel somewhat biased in their favor!

However, the reader is asked not to consider this little book as other than a compilation drawn from the accumulated wisdom of many business people. Only its method of presentation is "original." I did not invent the methods, though I have used them time and again to achieve my own definite purposes — which have had as a rule, little to do with the accumulation of money!

* * *

(I seem to hear some of my readers chuckle at this point with glee — "There you are! You were a failure, then, because your 'success' did not pay in money!" **BUT WAIT —**)

Feeling that no one is qualified to speak of the laws of business success with authority, unless they have personally succeeded in business by application of those laws, — before giving this little book over to the public, I did just that thing. I tell of it here, not in a spirit of boastfulness but merely to fortify the value of the lessons in other minds, by assurance that their author has demonstrated every "rule" laid down, although their time, energy and inclinations are far more pleasantly occupied when engaged in other than "business" pursuits.

Even to the point of "accumulating money," I now know from personal experience that the natural law of success works in business as infallibly as it has worked in whatever other lines of endeavor I have engaged in. At the present time I have four "business offices" and carry on several distinct "businesses," all of which are succeeding and bid fair to double in financial results each year. Within less than a year, for example, I tripled my personal income, which I consider a fairly reasonable demonstration.

This little personal interlude, though rather distasteful to me, seems to be necessary, in order to explain my chief motive in publishing this book. The motive of the book is to help others. If there is any financial profit in it, I won't certainly object — for that is "business."

But monetary returns enter not at all into the motive for presenting my readers a text that seems to be needed in the field of business psychology. I would be entirely willing to turn over any profits from sales to the furtherance of other good works. And dear reader, when you have remade yourself into a "business success," through this set of directions, if you have similar feelings with regard to part of your profits, suppose we talk it over. There is something greater even than success in business.

3

LESSON I

ATTENTION

Look up the word "Attention" in all the dictionaries and encyclopedias at your command. Read carefully and closely all that is said on the subject.

You will find that Attention is a mental faculty that enables you to concentrate your power of observation or thought on anything you choose and hold it steadily before your "mind's eye" so that you may study it, analyze it, classify its parts and arrive at definite conclusions about it.

These conclusions you file away in your memory with a feeling of confidence that they can be recalled as clear-cut impressions of definite, mental experience. Under the subject of Memory (Lesson 7) more will be said of this.

Here, we discover that Memory is but an evidence of the degree of Attention.

A few experiments will quickly convince you of the truth of this statement.

(a). In the quiet of your den, take up a law report, for example, note the title, (say California Report 65), turn to the fifth case reported, note the page and title of the case (say page 74, State of California vs. James White), then read the syllabus.

You will find you do not accomplish this in a manner to be able to remember it all clearly and accurately. When you find where you slipped a cog, go back and examine attentively wherein you are at fault and correct yourself. Repeat this sort of exercise daily and you will discover that you progress further and further until you are able to remember every detail of a lengthy and complicated report at the first reading.

(b). In your walks along the streets of your town or out in the country, take careful note of everything you pass. Afterward see how many of them you can remember. Invariably you will have the clearest memories of those things to which you gave the most intense and undivided attention. This exercise was one of the secrets by which Robert Houdin, once the greatest of French stage magicians at the turn of the 20th century, built up his marvelous powers. It will repay you to read his autobiography should you run across it in some old library (or perhaps this author will reproduce it.)

Attention, then, is analogous to the microscope. Unlike the microscope, however, its power is unlimited so far as we know. The longer we focus it on an object, the more we see of the thing under consideration. Once we get the object under our microscope, it seems automatically to enlarge our powers of mental vision by a series of "adjustments" of focus, until we find out all we wish to know about the object and have secured micro-photographs of every phase of it to store away in memory.

It is not so easy to control Attention, however, as you may think. It requires as much time and skill as to become a good microbiologist using a microscope as part of their daily research (we will return to the analogy of a microscope often.) If you think you have more than the average ability to concentrate your Attention upon a single thing for any length of time, try it.

Endeavor to "concentrate" for example on a pencil, for say, five minutes, to the exclusion of everything else. If you can do it, you have remarkable ability for a beginner. If you can do this for half an hour, you are a mental wizard!

What happens is usually this:

A dozen sights, sounds, smells, or other stimuli to your nerves, distract your Attention. You force the withdrawal of your Attention from these distractions and focus it on the pencil — and again these disturbances scatter your Attention. At last you succeed in shutting out the sights and sounds and all other physical distractions, by the simple expedient of retiring to your den for Silence (see Lesson 4) but your Attention then is distracted by other thoughts than the thought of the pencil. A whole flock of thoughts arise, each one demanding some part of your Attention!

Why is this?

NORMAL DISTRIBUTION OF ATTENTION

Because in ordinary, daily life, Attention is necessarily divided between a great number of objects and impressions on consciousness. They become "matters of course"; we do not consider we are thinking of them at all. This distribution of Attention is as natural as the distribution of sunlight — and just as necessary to life.

We use a lens to concentrate the sunlight.

We use willpower to concentrate Attention.

From this we conclude that Attention not only serves us as a mental microscope, but that it is in some way connected with a source of mental light. We find a similarity between physical light and these mental rays (which are focused by Will), that leads us to suspect they both obey the same law, though perhaps on widely separated planes of being.

Our suspicions are well founded, for by further experiment we find that the source of mental light is that thing we call "Memory" (see Lesson 7); that those mental rays alluded to, which seem to shed their light on whatever we focus Attention, proceed from this central sun of Memory; and that this central sun itself is constantly fed with more light and energy from without through the process of Attention.

That is, we find that Attention both gives and receives. It surpasses the mechanical microscope or the "super microscope" by being its own generator of light. It is, in truth, an intelligent microscope.

WHY "BUSINESS" GETS CONFUSED

Instead of looking at a pencil, let us focus Attention on our business affairs. At first, unless we are already trained in efficient business methods, our affairs seem to be in more or less confusion. Like the little, microscopic animals in a drop of water, when we view our personal business affairs with **ATTENTION** we see the business of the home and its relations with the landlord, the butcher, the grocer, the laundry and so on; the business of our bread and butter job; the business of keeping clothed and fed; the business of possible investments; of taxes; of politics; of our social and religious and fraternal relations — all so closely related and so "mixed up" with each other, that we are inclined to grow discouraged wondering how the "tangle" ever got that way and how we are going to get it untangled.

The average human seems so distracted mentally by a multiplicity of "business" responsibilities that they gradually become unfit to attend to all of them and feels "lucky" if they "get past" with their job of earning a salary or wages. This is because their Attention is rarely, if ever, concentrated upon any single responsibility for any definite time. Instead, as they realize their responsibilities more and more, rather than rejoice at the opportunity they give for a greater display of efficient power in discharging them, they begin either to "worry" over them or to shirk from them.

There is no scientific reason why any human, of ordinary intelligence, should be "worried" save for an inability to "collect ones thoughts" — to "concentrate" their attention on the thing immediately before them.

We "worry" because we lack self-confidence. We fear our own knowledge is too small for the task required; our ability less than demanded. In plain English, we are afraid of ourselves. We know in our hearts that we are trying to bluff the world, including ourselves and are too lazy to make good the bluff. But we also know in some strange, intuitive fashion, that if we were not constitutionally lazy, and that if we "set our minds to it," we could overcome any obstacle in our path. That knowledge is the thing that makes us uncomfortable — the thing that we sometimes refer to as "conscience" (a word meaning "with knowledge").

So we continue to "worry" and worrying still further scatters our Attention — among the objects "worried" about.

Humankind becomes inefficient in their job to the extent they allow their attention to wander from it. They grow efficient to the extent they gather the "rays" of Attention and focus them upon their job.

HOW NOT TO WORRY

You can conquer worry, simply by devoting every ounce of energy and attention you have to whatever task you happen to be engaged upon at the time. Do your level best all the time. If your task is digging ditches, put all your "steam" into every ditch you dig — While you are digging it. If you are amusing yourself or others, devote your entire Attention to amusement and recreation — while you are at it. Don't permit a single thought about digging ditches, or paying debts, or anything past or future, to interfere.

KEEP YOUR MIND ON THE PRESENT TASK ALWAYS

If you feel bound to "worry" over something, set aside an hour per day as your "worrying" hour, and attend strictly to the business of worrying — during that hour only, until the absurdity of it cures you. Make the job of "worrying" a thorough one, while you are about it. Ransack your memory for things to "worry" about until you have exhausted your supply of "worrys" (misspelling is intentional to indicate distinct and separate units of worry.) In the end you will become wise with the wisdom of the ancients who first agreed there is "no use crying over spilled milk."

The successful business person is the one, who so controls this Attention that they can focus it on their business for as long as necessary to accomplish any given task or result. Perhaps your Attention has never been fully upon your business. You wonder at the seemingly unjust verdict of others on your work — Proof that Attention has strayed off into "wonder." You marvel that others with not half your intelligence get promoted over you — another proof that your Attention has been scattered. You fail to realize that the "other person" focused their **ENTIRE** attention on the task of getting ahead. Their intelligence and energy may have been much less than yours, but they were just wise enough to make the most of what they had. You wasted your efforts by scattering them.

Picture to yourself a great power station supplying light, heat and power say to a dozen cities. For some reason, the whole of the power generated is temporarily required to accomplish a certain work at the plant itself. So long as it is distributed throughout a dozen cities, obviously it cannot be concentrated at the plant. But it is a simple matter for the engineers in charge to shut off the power temporarily from every city and convey it, through a single huge conductor to the place where its own work is to be done. This may require but a few minutes — after which the power can be again distributed to the dozen cities.

HOW TO FOCUS ATTENTION

So it is with Attention. You can withdraw it at will from all else but the immediate task to be accomplished and direct it wholly toward the accomplishment of that task.

You may have a great number of tasks awaiting accomplishment. If your affairs are in a "tangle," you can untangle them very speedily, simply by giving each one your whole Attention until that task is finished — then pass to the next task and finish that and so on.

It is true that you cannot give your entire attention to several things at one time — you can only divide attention between them. But the human mind has no known limitation in the number of things to which its Attention may be directed, either by division of Attention between them all simultaneously, or by concentration on one thing at a time.

Every impression on consciousness receives a part of your Attention whether the impression is made on Self-consciousness (so that **YOU** yourself is aware of it) or on Sub-consciousness (so that **YOU** is not actively aware of it). This fact impresses us with a sense of the almost limitless power we can exert when we are able to focus our entire Attention on one thing.

There are successful business people that are directors in many companies to which they seem to "pay no attention." Or, they carry on successfully two or more distinct kinds of business every day. Yet they seem entirely care free — sometimes a bit contemptuous of people of less ability who invariably think they would have more if just "given a chance." How do these people do it?

They focus their whole attention on whatever is before them for the time necessary to accomplish it. How long this may take depends upon the nature of the work to be done and the mental alertness of the thinker.

THE TIME ELEMENT

There are 24 hours in the day. Nature requires 8 hours for rest and relaxation. There remain 16 hours in which one may accomplish whatever one wills — Be it business or pleasure. Most great captains of industry actually work the whole 16 hours, either physically or mentally. It is up to you as to how you divide your time — but you have at least 16 hours at your disposal.

A physical worker should average no more than 8 hours daily — physical work. For that, too, seems to be Nature's rule. And here the average human stops.

Suppose, however, a person devoted the remaining 8 hours to mental work — to concentrating their Attention on learning how to do their physical work better; to learning another trade or profession; to solving those of their problems for which the period they devoted to physical labor afforded them no time. You will need no great imagination to picture the result. That individual necessarily would "get ahead." They couldn't keep themselves down very well, and certainly no one else could.

USING THE BRAIN ONLY

There is a certain person of my acquaintance who is president and manager of a large manufacturing concern employing scores of people; they are also a very fine amateur artist and connoisseur, for whose work art collectors have offered huge sums; this individual is noted as a consulting engineer and gets hundreds of dollars an hour when employed; they are an inventor; a lecturer on legal subjects as well as on architecture, painting, and sculpture; this person likewise writes for magazines and is an author of some note. This individual receives and answers an average of 500 letters/emails every week dealing with 17 different lines of thought.

And yet, this person has never walked a step in their life. This person is a hopeless cripple, unable to move their legs the fraction of an inch and scarcely able to move the rest of their body save for their head and their hands from the wrist. In this individual's youth, they had a few months' of schooling and for years were unable to earn more than minimum wage each week. Today however, this person is a very wealthy, splendidly educated, and a widely honored citizen, sought out by their political party, their church and clubs for positions of responsibility. What was the secret of their rise to power, you may ask?

ATTENTION — CONCENTRATED ATTENTION

This person knew what they wanted to be and realized that by making use of what they had, they could accomplish their own desires. This individual devoted years of attention to learning things by observation, through books, and through talking with others who knew. This person used their 16 hours a day to good advantage. Now they work 17 hours applying that knowledge.

Yet all they ever had in their life to work with, were their brain and vital energy. This person's voice and the slight movement Nature has left in their hands, are their only physical means of expression. They are a Master Director — and so can employ others with strong bodies to execute their plans.

By **ATTENTION** we may discover all our own faults and destructive tendencies and so be enabled to correct them.

Obviously, if we have no knowledge of the business in which we are engaged or expect to be engaged, the mere exercise of Attention is wasted effort. We must have something definite upon whom to focus Attention. In such a case we should focus our Attention on our lack of knowledge, find out exactly what it is we lack — and then devote Attention to supplying the deficiency.

Knowledge is gained only by personal experience and observation through the medium of the senses.

But if one fails to give their personal experiences and observations more than casual Attention, they will not get far in reducing them to knowledge. They will "forget" things, because they retain only hazy outlines of impressions made by them on their consciousness. Consequently, they will be deficient in knowledge and inefficient in application of knowledge to the extent they "forget" or "do not know."

It then becomes apparent that Attention is the most important part of one's Self-conscious mechanism, through which impressions on the general consciousness are converted into items of personal knowledge. And so we are again brought into direct touch with Memory as an essential to success in business. (See Lesson 7.)

CONSCIOUSNESS SUBJECT TO EVOLUTION

Consciousness is a universal attribute of Nature which is transformed to Individual Consciousness in Humankind. Every atom, cell, organ or group of cells or organs in a person's mechanism is endowed with Consciousness. Humanity, as an individualized part of the universal consciousness (which is **INTELLIGENT** consciousness) is a center or focus of the same.

Within this human focus of consciousness, are various evolutionary stages broadly classed under the heading of Subconsciousness — or that part of human consciousness not yet actively and completely "individualized." That part, which is actively and completely individualized we call **SELF-CONSCIOUSNESS**. Self-consciousness is the director of all below it, for it is the person themselves. The great American inventor Thomas A. Edison was of the opinion that this **SELF** is made up of about 5 per cent only of the whole conscious intelligence of the entire human body.

Be that as it may, it would probably be a safe assumption in the business world that the same percentage holds true between the "workers" and the "directors" of business. And the percentage is dependent entirely upon the use people make of Attention.

SELF-CONSCIOUSNESS

Self-consciousness is that active and purposeful concentration of the general consciousness of Humanity that belongs peculiarly to humans and is in fact so thoroughly their own personal property that it cannot be taken away from them or destroyed without destroying their personality. Self-consciousness results from a very high coordination of the cell consciousness and the group consciousness of a person's own being.

It is the final effort of Nature to endow the individual with a mechanism capable of focusing all their powers in what we call **ATTENTION** (self-conscious attention) for the one purpose of helping Nature in her process of individualizing intelligence.

With this delicate instrument of the mind, we can focus Attention on whatever we desire within the range of our sensory organism, physical or mental. We can even peer down into passive, latent "Subconsciousness" and convert its stores of knowledge to active "Self-conscious" use.

SUB-CONSCIOUSNESS

Sub-consciousness is a vast storehouse for experiences, to many of which we have never given Self-conscious Attention, and therefore we do not our-**SELVES** really know anything about them. We know no more of the contents of this storehouse than we do of a library of books we have accumulated, but the larger part of which we have never read. Only the books we have read and remember do we know the contents of.

Every cell in our body has consciousness upon which impressions are made. But each cell and group of cells (organs, glands, nerves and so on) first attends strictly to its own immediate business of reacting to (and therefore recording) the impression made upon it. If the cell or group of cells happens to be directly connected with your perceptive center (which is in the middle of your head in the part of the brain containing the pineal gland and pituitary body) then **YOU** will feel, see, hear, taste or smell the impression, according to the nature of the vibration or stimulus making it.

We know something about the various special nerves of sense adapted to certain ranges of vibration. We have the power to concentrate our Attention on "hearing" by withdrawing Attention from the other senses — And thereby make our hearing apparently more acute for the time being. So we appear to "see more" or to detect very faint odors, or to touch, or "feel" extremely minute movements of matter or "waves" of energy — by simply concentrating our attention upon them. It is interesting to devise and try experiments for yourself along this line.

THE BUSINESS HUNCH

Anything that will induce you to cultivate your powers of Attention is helpful in promoting your business ability. For about 95 per cent of the cells and groups of cells in your body, although possessed of consciousness and memory, (through which are collected and stored the records of all past experiences and inherited tendencies), are so indirectly connected by nerve channels with the perceptive center of **SELF**, that **YOU** know next to nothing about them or their knowledge.

YOU have never given them particular attention. **YOU** have never learned to control them nor to make intelligent use of their knowledge. In fact, **YOU** have left them to attend to their own affairs, and they have done so in what appears to **YOU** an automatic fashion. Occasionally you have what you call a "Hunch" to do a certain thing, but cannot tell why you have it. But the "Hunch" say, turns out well, and you consider you have been "Lucky" in business.

It is a thing you rarely reason about — consequently, your mysterious "Hunches" sometimes fail to work to your advantage. The "Hunch" comes from that realm of your own passive, latent or Subconscious domain to which you ordinarily give no Attention. Women call it "Intuition."

As a matter of fact, we really "feel," and for a fleeting fraction of time are, Self-conscious perhaps, of the greater part of impressions on our general consciousness — That is, we are, for a moment self-consciously aware of them. They receive, however, but brief and imperfect Attention — so little that it seems to us as though the thing felt never happened.

But if we focus our Attention on the thing at the time, it happens, we find that a clear-cut mental impression or "memory," is made and filed away for future reference. As we rarely know or can be expected to know, at the time of the event, whether a memory of it will ever be useful to us in the future, the best rule to observe is to give all our impressions serious consideration and a reasonable amount of attention — sufficient attention to make them active Self-conscious possessions, rather than leave them to the obscurity of passive Subconsciousness.

Every "memory" is a Subconscious thing of course because Sub-consciousness is the storehouse of Memory. If left undisturbed by **YOU** with your powers of Self-conscious Attention, the cells and cell groups where these memories are stored, will go on attending strictly to their own business as long as your body is alive, without any thought of you as their Master — until they get into some trouble, they cannot manage for themselves (such as hunger or a quarrel with outside things) which upset their natural good health and freedom of action.

Then they set up a commotion that suddenly forces itself upon **YOUR** Attention and **YOU** know that some part of your machinery is out of order. If you have been so foolish as to neglect informing yourself about your own physical and mental make-up, you become worried — perhaps frightened at these messages from your unexplored possessions. You consult a doctor or a psychiatrist and submit yourself to their experimental methods of a cure. You lose time and efficiency.

HOW TO KEEP HEALTHY

The business of keeping your mind and body in good health is therefore merely a matter of Attention to their demands. But it is as important a job as earning wages or getting a commercial transaction finished. Without an efficient mechanism your personal affairs in all directions will suffer. You should therefore use **ATTENTION** in keeping your mind and body fit.

Remember, however, you cannot give your full Attention to more than one thing at a time. This means that to be 100 per cent efficient in whatever you undertake, you should divide your time and not your attention.

One task at a time should be your rule. It may take days or years to finish a task, and you may be able to devote only one hour a day to it. But during that one hour devote your entire attention to it. Let no other task and no other thought but of the work in hand interfere with the accomplishment of that hour.

You will have desires and ambitions to do many things. But they must not be permitted to distract Attention from the immediate work you are doing. Assign them definite hours for a "hearing." Keep office hours on your Ambitions, your thoughts, your desires, your work. That is business. That is system.

No business person would permit a friend to interrupt a business conference with their associates in some "deal" by talking golf or some other unrelated business. Nor will they let "business" intrude on a serious golf game.

Efficient people are those who attend strictly to the work before them and concentrate their whole Attention upon the thing being done. Efficiency naturally attracts efficiency. The business superiors of an efficient individual are looking out for such as those to help them in their own tasks and responsibilities.

They may not promote this person as a matter of philanthropy, but they will certainly do so for their own interests when they are convinced of their efficiency. They must do so as a matter of "good business." The efficient person may not be known where they are needed and wanted. But again "Attention" comes to the rescue and promotion is won by giving Attention to the job of advertising one's efficiency to those in position to give promotion.

Advertising always pays — but it must be efficient advertising.

You must "have the goods" and then the power of concentrating your Attention on the effort to convince others you "have the goods."

The whole purpose of the business world is to enable a person through their own efforts to achieve financial independence for themselves and their family by exchanging their service for the service of others, so that they may be an efficient and happy member of that world. Every person is under an obligation to themselves and society to achieve this desirable condition. Attention is the very first essential to success.

PRACTICE THE FOLLOWING EXERCISE DAILY

Attention — Concentrate your attention upon everything that transpires from the time you get up in the morning until say, you reach your place of work: in the following manner.

(a). I awake; I stretch and feel better; I get up — Take exercise, say Walter Camp's Daily Dozen; I count each of the dozen, noting carefully the increasing alertness of mind and body as the blood circulates and the muscles get limbered up; I note just what muscles and what locations in my body seem to feel invigorated first. While taking these exercises I think of nothing but them. Instantly I cease them; I cease to think of them and turn my attention to — .

(b). Dressing. I note the shape, cleanliness, general condition of each article of clothing I put on. I note just which article comes first, and which next, and so on. I count the buttons as I fasten them. Mentally I record each act of dressing — if there is a clock convenient, I note the exact time it takes me to dress. I endeavor to look neat; business like. The instant I finish dressing I give it no further thought, my attention being directed to the next immediate activity of the morning, which, for example, may be

(c). Breakfast. The nature of the call to breakfast interests me: a bell, a gong, a voice calls me; is it a cheerful sound? — that is, does the person calling me to breakfast indicate through that call a cheerful frame of mind, or one tired of routine or irritable from any cause? If irritable, why? Have I been at fault to make it so? Would a display of cheerfulness, of vigor, of energy, on my part, change things? Is my appearance and general atmosphere such as to make my presence at breakfast welcome? Mentally I count my steps to the table; my address to others there or who may come after me is deliberately calculated to inspire geniality, liking. Carefully I note the appearance, odor, taste, amount, of all I eat, endeavoring to classify the things that give me most pleasure and the reasons, therefore; the sequence in which they come and are eaten; the remarks of myself and others at the table. I am attentive when others talk; definite when I talk myself and careful that nothing I may say or do leave behind an unpleasant feeling. Breakfast is an experience —-a series of experiences — to be enjoyed if possible; to furnish me energy for the work that is to come. The instant it is finished I give it no more thought, but turn my attention to the next thing, say

(d). The trip to work. I say goodbye to my family, with attention to the act of leaving that will give pleasure to them and to myself in the remembrance of it. Those I meet on the way, that I know, I greet in the same spirit. Especially if one is downcast, depressed, I endeavor to override their depression with my own cheerfulness.

I note attentively all that I pass on the way to work as thoroughly as the speed at which I travel will permit. I look in store windows, at signs, at people, as at a panorama, noting how one thing follows another and the instant memory of other things it arouses. Then I am at my place of work. The moment I enter I dismiss all thought of my trip from home and turn my attention exclusively toward my work.

At night, when I am back home and have a brief period of quiet just before retiring, I check up on the morning's exercise in Attention, which checking up is an exercise in **MEMORY**, as you will find under that title to follow.

4

LESSON II

ATTITUDE

Your personal viewpoint in life is the next essential factor in business success, or in success of any kind. Upon your general Attitude, depend upon the direction your efforts toward success will take.

Attention by itself is therefore useless unless you aim it in the right direction. A hunter may load their gun perfectly and "concentrate" enough powder and shot (in the form of the right caliber of a bullet) in the charge to kill an elephant. Should they fire it off at random? no shot would be likely to hit the mark.

By **"ATTITUDE"**, it is meant one's individual relation to their work and fellow workers. It is peculiar to themselves alone. Everyone who would succeed in financial affairs or in business finds it necessary to maintain a definite mental attitude toward their "bread and butter" job: toward money and the use of money: toward employers or employees; toward the economic system created by society and civilization: and toward humanity and "the business world" in general.

Our Attitude is too often rather a vague — indefinite — wavering stance. No wonder we rarely hit anything. Others see our errors and inconsistencies more quickly than ourselves, but we can discover and also correct these faults by giving the problem Attention. Self-analysis is the surest cure for bad aim!

It is on the subject of **ATTITUDE** that so many instructors in "Applied Psychology"' confuse the student by remarks of this kind:

"Simply hold the thought and what you want will come to you."

"Applied psychology really abolishes work."

"If you want money, get in harmonious vibration with it and hold the thought — money will come."

These are mystical rather than scientific statements. If understood literally they are mere absurdities. They all refer to the problem of **ATTITUDE** without giving any real information or hint of the truth.

You can't "abolish work" simply by thinking. But you can change your mental Attitude toward work until it is no longer disagreeable labor, but actually becomes a pleasure — indeed, a necessity to you.

Sitting around at your leisure and thoughtfully "vibrating" over a matter of thousands or millions of dollars you want will not get you a red cent. You may "hold the thought" that it will "come to you" until you are black in the face and it will not budge. But if you want money, you can get it by combining a personal effort with your thoughts. Money "vibrates" too fast for a lazy individual to collect much of it. Business people say money "circulates" rather than "vibrates."

The cold scientific fact is that unless the worker is in harmony with their work, they are not happy. If they are not happy in their work, they are not thoroughly efficient. If they are not efficient, they cannot be a success. Hence, they must adopt an attitude toward their work that will put them and it in "harmony."

ARE YOU IN HARMONY WITH YOUR WORK? IF NOT, WHY?

To say your work is personally distasteful to you is not a sufficient answer. It may be all work is distasteful to you, which is only another way of saying that you are just plain **LAZY**.

Find work that is personally agreeable, give it your undivided attention then succeed.

An Attitude of Aversion to all work makes you completely negative to success in business. Society would be much better off without you, for you are like a dead cell in the living body of humanity. You obstruct the channels through which its life forces must flow.

If you have such an Attitude, it is obvious that you are aiming in exactly the opposite direction from the object you desire to shoot at. Your problem, therefore, is to find the target, draw a bead on it, then fire your gun — You can't miss.

Your target is the **WORK** that you do best and that you like best.

Self-analysis is about the only way to locate this target.

HOW TO QUESTION YOURSELF

ATTENTION, remember, is the microscope to be used in analyzing yourself.

Here are some suggestions to which you may profitably turn your Attention:

1. What are your Emotions with respect to your trade or profession and why do you have them? (Refer to Lesson 6 on Emotion.)

2. Is there a particular trade or profession you feel you are fitted for and would find less distasteful than others? What is it? Why?

3. What sort of work, if any, do you most desire to do? Why?

4. What sort of work are yon best trained or fitted for? Why?

5. Have you any aspirations or ambitions? What are they with regard to a means of earning a living? Make the list as complete as yon can.

6. What incentives have you for earning a living by work? That is, have you dependents, loved ones? Would you enjoy helping others if in position to do so? Have you debts, and would you like to get them paid? These and others will suggest themselves, so make a complete list.

7. To what do you most aspire in life? By what means can you imagine that your aspiration may be achieved other than through personal effort? Why?

When you have carefully tabulated these questions and their answers you will have some very definite information about yourself that possibly every one of your acquaintances could have told you long ago, but which you would have resented coming from them. Yet you did not yourself realize the truth, because you would not give your Attention to the disagreeable facts.

It takes a degree of courage to indulge in this sort of self-analysis and carry it to a conclusion by comparing your own answers and adding up the results. The grand total is the Truth about yourself. The Truth then becomes an asset of incalculable value. You discover all your own shortcomings as well as your potentialities.

Knowing these, you know **WHAT** your Attitude should be in order to hit the target of success. This knowledge is worth all the hurt to your self-pride and the pain of injured vanity that self-analysis will cause you.

For illustration, we will suppose that your "grand total," when you balance accounts with yourself, is the usual one — **FEAR**.

You arrived at this probably unexpected answer as follows:

1. I dislike my job because the boss is selfish, tyrannical. My boss is liable to fire me at any time. The hours are too long and the pay poor. The work itself is pleasant enough if it were not that I am under the thumb of a money grubbing, unsympathetic old employer.

2. I am a clerk, but would rather be a traveling salesman, as this would give a chance for advancement and commissions.

3. Answered above.

4. I want something that will offer continuous opportunity for promotion, increased responsibility and pay.

5. I've a family to support; I want some authority of my own and to get out of a rut in which I may have to spend my whole life if something doesn't turn up. But then I always was an unlucky fellow. Opportunity never seems to come my way.

6. Answered above.

7. Partly answered above. I don't know any way of "making an honest living" except by work. Often I think, "what's the use" when I see rich people and powerful bosses getting away with big grafts. Yet the poor devils who steal a few pennies or have nerve enough to take it away from the rich ones get caught and put in jail.

This may be a bit overdrawn. But the sum total of it is **FEAR, DISTRUST, DISLIKE, SUSPICION, PREJUDICE**. These emotions crop out in every answer. Rather it is one aggregate of emotions that may be defined as LACK of **SELF CONFIDENCE**.

We **"FEAR"** poverty, ridicule, rebuffs, misunderstanding — merely because we lack Self-confidence. We secretly fear we haven't the ability, the knowledge, the courage to do a thing we intuitively **KNOW** should be done. And so, we are all, to some degree, cowards.

TO OVERCOME FEAR, CULTIVATE SELF-CONFIDENCE.

By continued self-analysis of the kind suggested, you will find either that your work is so unpleasant (because of faults that are not chargeable to you) that it is the part of wisdom to quit it and get a more pleasant occupation; or else that you can eliminate your own destructive emotions, establish your confidence in your own ability, achieve more pleasure in your work, become more efficient and thereby attract others to you rather than repel them.

If you are not making a success in business, despite your belief that you are giving your business affairs the strictest Attention, then there is assuredly something wrong with your Attitude.

You will discover by asking yourself **"WHY?"** to every answer in the course of self-analysis (until you can't ask Why any further) that you have failed to direct your Attention toward this problem of **ATTITUDE**.

NEVER SLIP OVER TROUBLE — MASTER IT

Never leave your personal problems partly unsolved, but give every phase of each problem an attentive examination. There is no such thing as an unsolvable problem. You will discover the solution if you concentrate your Attention on it, for Nature has placed the answer within you. It is bound to come out. If the answer wasn't there you would not be aware there was a problem.

NATURE NEVER PERMITS A SANE PERSON TO TAKE THE WRONG PATH WHEN

PROPER ATTENTION IS GIVEN TO HER ADVICE.

Nature demands that your whole Attitude towards your work should be one of personal interest. You must realize that whatever you engage in is **YOUR** work and not a job owned by someone else that is temporarily leased to you.

WORK "WITH" AND NOT "FOR" "THE BOSS."

GET YOUR EMPLOYEES TO WORK "WITH" AND NOT "FOR" YOU.

You may be unjustly treated by those with whom you work. You may be underpaid and over-bossed.

But so long as you have a "job" entrusted to your care, you have an obligation to yourself and the rest of humanity to accomplish it efficiently. The "job" is yours so long as you work at it, because you are a part of humanity and the job is part of the world's work. No job belongs to any individual save the person working on it.

Clever, competent, wise and industrious individuals create plans that call for a variety of jobs to put into execution. And we say they "create" these jobs. The strict truth is that Nature creates the jobs, and they all belong to Nature, who gives them to people to perform, who want to perform them.

When Sir Issac Newton discovered the law of gravity, he made no claim to have created it. He did not invent the consequences of the law. And so the builders of great commercial enterprises have planned machinery calling for workmen to operate it. But they did not invent or create the work any more than they invented or created the workmen.

You and your work may not suit each other, but remember that the work is **YOUR** particular "job" so long as you are in possession of it. If you do not fit each other, quit it and find something else to do more to your liking.

Remember: — **YOU ARE BUT A SINGLE CELL IN THE BODY OF HUMANITY. THE INSTANT YOU CEASE TO FUNCTION YOU ARE IN THE WAY — YOU MUST BE REMOVED, AND YOUR WORK MUST BE DONE BY SOME OTHER CELL OR CELLS OR THE WHOLE BODY SUFFERS.**

As you concentrate your attention on this fact and its implications, you find that your whole mental attitude undergoes a constructive change. Your relations with the entire world of things and people with whom you come into contact, appear in a light entirely new, and in which you have not heretofore seen them.

By such constant study, your "work" gradually assumes an importance it has never had before — you find positive pleasure in certain "work" for which you discover you are best fitted.

Only the recognition of **SYSTEM**, as a part of the natural law with which you are trying to align yourself, will enable you to rise in the business world. Every task must be performed thoroughly by you so long as it is your task. Then you are always prepared for advancement, promotion, opportunity.

Step by step, your Attention is directed or drawn forward.

Step by step, your Attitude points out the right direction for Attention to follow.

Let Attitude be one of Aversion to work and Attention will be constantly given to the causes of Aversion, magnifying them and seeking to have you cling closer to the negative, pessimistic, grouchy, fault-finding, suspicious and unhappy side of the world's work. Attention will merely feed Memory on every destructive emotion toward which your Attitude naturally turns it.

But let your Attitude be one of the enjoyments of your work — and, as the mystics say, you can "abolish work" — that is, transmute it into pleasurable "occupation."

Your Attitude has "polarized" your whole being, as it were, so that your own individual energies and the forces of Nature seem to flow through you and your machinery without discord and with very little resistance. You become a good conductor for intelligent energy.

When we say a thing is "polarized," we mean that all its particles are turned or tend to turn in one general direction. So, when we have achieved a correct Attitude toward our work and environment, all our thoughts and energies, and our Attention as well, turn that way and flow in that direction. We will grow in that direction ourselves.

The word that defines the correct Attitude for success in business, is **CHEERFULNESS.**

The business person who holds constantly and consistently the attitude of cheerfulness in all their work, thereby removes from their pathway virtually every adverse influence that could hinder their business success.

An individual of this type was hailed by a friend who wanted them to drop their business and play golf with them. This person replied cheerily: "I can't do it today — Have a pleasanter thing on hand."

"What is it?" their friend inquired.

"I'm going to meet a grouchy old customer on business."

This individual met their "old grouchiness," and closed a business deal that netted them the equivalent of about five years' good income. Later this person's friend asked them how they did it. They replied:

"He told me it was because I am 'such a consistently cheerful business idiot.'"

Because those willing to take risks seem to have this faculty of "making the best of everything" and of "taking things as they find them," they make the best and most intelligent people of business in the world. They are not cramped between the walls of "rule of thumb" and ironclad convention so much as are those of lesser drive. Their Imagination gives wings to their minds, and others scarcely know whether to condemn them as crazy or admire them for their daring. They do not understand.

As a group their attitude toward work is gradually becoming one that regards business as an exchange of Service, rather than a mere piling up of dollars.

PRACTICE THE FOLLOWING EXERCISE DAILY

Attitude — Select each day, upon beginning work, some part of that work, or some individual connected with it, that is not entirely agreeable to you. (If there are none such, you are fortunate, for then you have no problem of Attitude to solve.)

Select that which is less disagreeable first. Then say to yourself something like: "This thing or this person is not pleasing to me; I feel irritated, or depressed, or discouraged or in some manner not in harmony with it or them. This feeling impairs my own efficiency, whether it is my fault or that of the other person or thing. I cannot permit myself to be injured, for when I am inefficient, I am not worth to myself or others what I know I am worth as an efficient worker. Hence my Attitude toward the person or thing must in some manner be changed at once, or in justice to myself I must get out of this environment and seek another more pleasant and harmonious one.

"Therefore, **WHY** do I have this feeling? Whose fault is it? If it is that of the thing I do, then I am obviously not fit for the work, because work, in itself, has no possible grudge or ill feeling toward me. Hence, it is better for me to seek other work I like. I will do this work thoroughly today, give it the most concentrated attention — just as an experiment — to discover if it is true that I do not like it and that it is the thing that is disagreeable instead of myself. It may be that I dislike it or seem to dislike it, because I have never really done it **ATTENTIVELY**. (You will be surprised what a difference it makes to do this.) After I have done the work thoroughly once, taken notes of each action, as well as the successful display of my skills... then should it still be disagreeable I will set about finding something else to do.

If the disagreeable association is a person, instead of a thing, I will first of all, endeavor with an impartial mind to discover how much, if any, of the hurtful feeling that impairs my efficiency, is my own fault. That much, at least, I can correct.

Why should I dislike the person? They are overbearing, a bully, a loud-mouthed boaster, or a coarse fellow whose actions jar on my supposedly finer sensibilities? Just how much finer are my sensibilities than theirs, and what do I judge by? Have I any other standard of judging them and their actions by than — **MYSELF?** Am I justified in judging them by myself? Does the fellow so impress my other fellow workers? Why? Are my standards so much higher than theirs — **WHY?** If I resent personally their actions that are not addressed to me, am I not interfering with their freedom, as I would not have them interfere with me (and mine)?

This sort of self-analysis may go far toward changing your attitude of Aversion towards the person.

But, assuming that you bring about within yourself that degree of tolerance and willingness to cooperate that makes for a proper Attitude on your part, and yet you cannot like the other individual, however much you try and also assuming that there are fundamental differences in your character and theirs that just will not harmonize to bring about this liking, you can then protect yourself from the destructive emotion of active dislike — simply by withdrawing your Attention from the person. Ignore them in the sense that you do not permit what they say or do, to arouse any emotions in you. Be polite, be courteous, be ever ready to serve them in the interest of your common work, but in nothing else give them any attention. Let them be to you as any other object which does not especially interest you. Make a habit daily of cultivating Attitude in this manner.

5

LESSON III

ENERGY

When someone gains the Attention of others through the force of their own personality, we say they have "Personal Magnetism," or that they have a "Magnetic Personality."

It is a quality instantly recognized and is built up through the adoption of the right Attitude toward one's work and fellow workers. We know the "magnetic" individual succeeds in life where the colorless, negative, pessimistic fellow fails.

There is "something" about the individual with a "Magnetic Personality" that everyone feels drawn to. You want to be in their company; to do business with them in preference to others; to be their friend and to have them for your friend.

This "something" is a real mental force — an energy we may give any name we please, just so we use it intelligently. It is our "Life force," when it is under control of our Will and doing what our Will demands of it.

Physicians call it "Vital Energy," and tell us that it flows off the ends of severed nerves and depletes our strength during an operation, so that we suffer from shock and physical exhaustion, quite as much when we are under an anesthetic and do not at the time "feel" pain, as when we feel all the agony of the shock.

It is therefore called, "Nerve force" or nervous energy, by some because the nerves are its conductors much as copper wires conduct electricity, or a bit of iron will serve as a magnet and maintain around itself a "magnetic field."

Some electro-chemists speak of this mental force as "human electricity." Others seem inclined to use an old term from as far back as the eighteenth century, "human magnetism"; but no matter what theories or beliefs or disbeliefs we have about it, or what name we choose to give this energy, we instinctively recognize two things about our own supply of it:

1. Plenty of vital energy means health and strength.

2. An insufficient supply causes us to feel physically weak and mentally depressed.

In the first instance we incline toward a feeling that we can sweep any obstacle aside that hampers our success. In other words, when we are "filled with energy," we have a sense of our own power we do not have when the supply is below normal — "Self-confidence."

This feeling of power is not "just a dream." It is actual knowledge gained by every part of your working mechanism of mind and body, telling you, "We are in condition and filled with motive-power to accomplish whatever you demand."

So, the possession of plenty of Vital Energy creates a natural tendency in you to adopt the correct Attitude for success.

This is a most important fact for you to realize, because by responding to this natural tendency, in order to do what you must, you must first build up your health and strength – you work with Nature and aid her to aid you. Your Attitude towards your work and toward the world in general, will become all that Nature demands, simply by following her suggestions. This will impel you to a cheerful and optimistic view of life, no matter what the apparent difficulties that confront you. Thereby you become a "Magnetic Personality."

It is probable that most successful business people use their Vital energy in this "magnetic" manner, subconsciously. How much more efficient they would be could they use it self-consciously!

WHERE IT COMES FROM

Let us analyze this potent force, so that our use of it may be intelligent and self-conscious.

What is "Vital Energy" — or whatever you wish to term the life force?

It is derived largely from the food, air and drink we take into the body. Therefore, it must be a combination of all other energies, lower than that of human life. These are digested and transformed within the body into an energy suitable for operating the machinery of mind and body, somewhat in the manner coal energy is transformed into steam power or electricity by mechanical processes.

It is unimportant here to consider the laboratory experiments by which scientists have determined the nature of human energy to be such that we may regard it as something as tangible as other forces which we store and use to accomplish our work.

But it is important to bear in mind the fact that human energy may be generated, "bottled," released at will, and otherwise utilized to accomplish specific results, even more effectively than steam, electricity, magnetism, light, heat, radiation, or any other form of energy with which mankind is now acquainted or is ever likely to be acquainted. This is because human vital energy embraces all other energies and is above them all. It is an **INTELLIGENT** energy. And we are its masters.

All this is done inside our bodies, however. Every cell of the body is a storage battery. The nerves are the wires that connect these batteries. The whole effect of this system of storage of energy is to provide us with an "energy body" as it were, in the sense we speak of a "nerve body," a "muscular body," or "bony skeleton."

THIS ENERGY BODY MAY BE SET IN MOTION BY AN IMPULSE OF THE WILL, SO THAT DEFINITE CURRENTS OF ENERGY MAY BE SET FLOWING IN WHATEVER DIRECTION WE WISH IT TO ACCOMPLISH WORK.

Currents of energy are constantly flowing in definite directions through the body, set up by the motions of the heart, lungs and other organs, with which every one is familiar — such as the energy which flows with the blood stream; or currents which flow to and from the brain carrying impressions derived through the sensory nerves.

But when we **THINK**, currents of energy are also set in motion. To illustrate: Scientists tell us that some two-thirds of our blood is required in the stomach after meals in order to digest the food we have eaten. Hence, the energy of two-thirds of our blood cells is there.

ENERGY FOLLOWS ATTENTION

They also tell us, when we engage in thought or "brain work" that two-thirds of the blood (and its energy) rushes to the brain, where it is needed to carry on the work being done there.

It will now be clear to you why concentrated Attention has the effect of concentrating your energy.

If you doubt this, try the following experiment:

Take your most important business problem to the quiet of your room, and concentrate your entire attention upon it for as long as you can. When the strain grows greater than you, feel you can stand any longer, relax entirely and turn your attention to the results.

You will probably note at once a sense of relief, of exhaustion. Your feet are cold or clammy. You perspire freely at the temples or over the face, neck and scalp. A brief rest, however, seems to restore your strength in the rest of the body.

All of which goes to show that during the time your Attention is concentrated on one thing, your Energy is drawn in part at least from every part of your body. When Attention is released from its temporary confinement and redistributed in its usual channels, so is your Energy.

When we "Will" to do a thing, we give a mental push to the energy of the brain cells in the neighborhood of the place we "Will" from — wherever that is. This push releases energy to the next cells and so on until the message has reached whatever part of our body it is intended for where the command is carried out by our intelligent mechanism and an answer returned informing us of the fact.

The nerves are the special conductors of these commands, and if they are broken, pinched or withered, the message cannot reach the part intended. Our machinery may lack some of its parts, such as legs or arms, and therefore be of no use to us. But these things are not insurmountable obstacles to success when we know how to use our energy.

They merely deprive us of the use of physical means of expression — not of the energy to do work. The same energy can be utilized to operate whatever machinery we have and not being needed in the defective or missing parts, can be more strongly concentrated wherever it will be most effective.

If we are unable, because of special conditions to direct our energy through one channel, we have only to find another available channel and direct it there. It is not the conductor of energy that is important, but getting it to the place where work is to be done.

Experience teaches that there are many obstacles in the way of directing our energy with 100 per cent efficiency. But all these can be overcome by intelligent effort.

People who have been deprived of the use of virtually every part of their physical machinery have become great executives, directing the physical work of hundreds of others to accomplish plans which perhaps not one of those individuals could have conceived.

WHAT OBSTRUCTS ENERGY

What is 100 per cent efficiency in directing one's energy?

Obviously this would be the instant response of our entire energy to the demands of Will. And obviously, this cannot be obtained so long as any hindrance impedes the flow of energy.

Some of these hindrances are.

Ill health, which means that the mechanism of nerves and cells of the body is out of gear and therefore offers resistance to the normal flow of energy.

A wrong mental Attitude toward one's work or fellow-workers, which necessarily means that Attention is turned toward that which is destructive of success. And this means that Energy, which follows Attention will be turned toward destructive uses.

Bad habits, an argumentative disposition, stubbornness, egotism, vanity, and other mental dispositions offer resistance to the flow of energy quite as effectively as pinched nerve.

Up to this point, we have chiefly considered what goes on inside the body in relation to its energy and its control by Will Power. Now let us consider how it connects our interior, mental world with the outside world of matter and energy.

All matter is radioactive, not excepting the human life cell. Everything in Nature is constantly radiating energy — throwing it off into space. The human body does this to a greater extent than any other material form, because it is so constantly in action. Complete rest, implies complete equilibrium of forces and cessation of radioactivity. Movement is the thing that keeps energy radiating, because every change of position in a body brings it into new relations with everything surrounding it, and therefore upsets the equilibrium of energies between them, that may exist with all in a state of rest.

ENERGY RADIATES

Human radiations have been detected with a thermopile at a distance of several hundred feet, so we suggest nothing that has not been scientifically proven, when we say that human energy leaves the body at a terrific rate of speed under normal conditions though the different energies of various cells and groups of cells may vary in velocity.

The significance of this is, the human Body is a generator of power, a transformer of power and also a motor; that its unused surplus energy can be stored and directed for accomplishing work; and that its used energy and an oversupply of energy are given off by the body much as steam or electricity escapes from the machines they operate.

This escaping energy constitutes a conscious, intelligent link between us and the rest of the world of consciousness and intelligence. It surrounds us with a "Personal Atmosphere" much as the earth is enveloped in its own atmosphere. It is an atmosphere which other people with whom we come into contact actually "Feel" or "sense" — through their possession of the same envelope of energy.

How often have you heard perfectly sane and normal business people speak of an outstanding personality in some such words as these? "When I am in their presence, I feel drawn to them," or "You just have a sense of being in the presence of a dynamic personality."

Although few of us direct our attention to the reason for such impressions, we accept them as facts.

When we bear in mind that **THOUGHT** can set up motion and produce currents or "waves" or "vibrations" in our energy, the reason we have these strange feelings of attraction or repulsion in the presence of certain people becomes clear. We not only radiate a "Personal Atmosphere," but it carries with it an impress of our thoughts — that is it radiates our Attitude toward those we come in contact with and our Attitude toward other things in which that person has an interest. They feel our Attitude and we feel theirs.

That we do not recognize all this in a Self-conscious way, does not do away with the fact that it is so.

PERSONAL ATMOSPHERE

Our personal Atmosphere is as much a part of us as are our arms and legs. When we wish to make ourselves agreeable to another person, we give them a warm handshake and they are conscious of our good intentions from that handclasp. But we seldom approach others with our thoughts purposely charged with feelings of good will and friendship, which will have far greater effect in convincing others as to your intentions than the handclasp or handshake!

We all know people whose "magnetic" and "dynamic" personality enlivens any gathering where they may be. We do not have to touch their hands to feel this. Cheerfulness and optimism and energy seem to radiate from them as odor radiates from a flower — and it is actually so. On the other hand we are acquainted with those who radiate exactly the opposite impressions.

Hence, it is important for us to realize the fact that our Attitude cannot be camouflaged entirely, no matter how we may attempt to deceive ourselves. It really "Radiates from us."

We live in the collective, large atmosphere of our community. We literally become parts of the collective thought of a city, state or nation — because we live so close to each other our thoughts "touch" so to speak; what we think is in some measure beating upon the brain of other people and what they think is knocking at our brain. We live in an unseen world of flashing moving thoughts, radiating from the visible individual bodies of people in the seen world. Unless you become a hermit, you cannot escape this contact with the world's thought by which you and the rest of humanity learn from each other daily.

Great leaders in business often attribute their success to "knowledge of human nature," and how to use that knowledge in persuading others to their way of thinking. Upon examination of their methods, we find they used what is called the "dominant mind" in a crowd.

A "dominant mind" can be forceful and violent so that others will merely regard it as a bully and tyrant, or it can be persuasive by appealing to one's intellect. Successful business people are persuasive.

When approaching people with whom you expect to transact business, do so with the intent to make an agreeable impression — to leave a sense of your own self-confidence in your own power which you are ready to place at the service of whomsoever you deal with. Remember that business IS entirely a matter of giving and receiving **SERVICE**.

Such a being your **ATTITUDE** it will be felt by the individual approached and they will respond according to their own Attitude. It may be that your two Attitudes and therefore your Wills and Energies and everything about you, will at first conflict. But if you maintain the positive, constructive Attitude, described herein as one of "Cheerfulness" it will inevitably overcome any Attitude of lesser positive degree. Most certainly the negative destructive Attitude of "Aversion" must give way, however slowly.

Your Attitude actually both envelopes you and the person you are talking to; they do the same with you; the two Attitudes which freight your respective "Personal Atmospheres" interpenetrate each other, and it is merely a question as to which is the more positive and the better aligned with Nature's building up processes, as to which one will prevail. A victory by the business builder over their rival, strangely enough brings no real bitterness of defeat to them. For it is a victory of knowledge and power over ignorance and weakness. The defeated individual learns and profits when they lose to a real business builder.

Whatever your business, trade or profession, it is through this envelope of Personal Atmosphere, composed of radiating energy and thought, that you advertise yourself and the kind of service you render to others. Through it your **ATTITUDE** attracts the Attention of others, either to hold it or to lose it and repel them according as your Attitude is scientifically correct and natural or wrong and abnormal.

In this manner and by this method you can lay your wares before others and make known your desire pleasantly and agreeably, to people with whom you might otherwise have small chance of discussing them by word of mouth. You can make yourself an "outstanding personality", despite all efforts of others to prevent it, when all other channels of advertising are closed to you.

HOW TO CULTIVATE LATENT POWER

By close study of what qualities of character attract people engaged in the same work as your own, you can cultivate the right Attitude and radiate it to them, thereby attracting to you the attention of all who might be concerned in your advancement. They will meet you at least half way, business people are constantly in search of individuals who are efficient. They want them for employees, and they desire them as partners.

BUT, YOU MAY ASK, "WHAT IS MEANT BY CULTIVATING ONE'S LATENT POWERS?" Granting that everything said about using one's whole energy to cultivate Attention, Attitude and other things helpful to succeed in business, is true — **HOW SHOULD I GO ABOUT IT?**

THE ANSWER IS — YOU "CULTIVATE" A POWER BY CONSTANTLY USING IT.

To cultivate Attention, for example, you must make a frequent practice of examining things attentively. To cultivate an Attitude, you must think of it constantly and act upon the thought as constantly.

USE is Nature's method of strengthening. The more you use a muscle or the brain the stronger it becomes. **DISUSE** is the way to loss of energy. **USE** is the way to increase your supply. **USE** increases the capacity for energy. **DISUSE** decreases the capacity.

PRACTICE THE FOLLOWING EXERCISES DAILY

Energy — Since Attitude directs Energy, the following exercise it is assumed, you will undertake only when you have the **RIGHT** Attitude. Select each day, some part of your work or business, that you are most anxious to have succeed — some part that you know can be done within the day. Focus your entire attention upon it (which is to say your entire mental energy and whatever physical energy is necessary to accomplish it) and then **DO IT**.

For example — answer all your correspondence (emails, texts, and letters). Clear it off the desk, the computer, and the mobile. Do it thoroughly; finish it and file it away. No matter how mixed up it may be, arrange it in a pile — so to speak — and go through with it. Do nothing else but that, during the period of time you set aside for it. Expend your energy in bringing system out of chaos.

DO this daily with some item of work, no matter how slipshod you may discover yourself to be with regard to other things. The practice will create in you sub-consciously, a desire to do all things that way.

6

LESSON IV

SILENCE

The most successful business people are those who work silently — and advertise most.

Here is a seeming paradox that needs explanation.

SILENCE IS A CONSERVATOR OF ENERGY.

NOISE IS A WASTER OF ENERGY.

ON THE AMOUNT OF ENERGY WE CAN BRING TO BEAR UPON OUR WORK DEPENDS OUR DEGREE OF SUCCESS.

Hence, the business person who is silently efficient, most strongly attracts the attention of others to their efficiency. Their very silence is their best advertisement — the trademark and badge of their efficiency.

The best advertisement in the world is the truthful one — free from extravagant claims, boasting or misrepresentation. The silent advertiser inspires confidence because they convince the purchaser of their wares that they "have the goods" by actually showing them and letting the purchaser be their own judge.

As the old adage says, "the individual of words and not of deeds" is the person who inspires distrust.

HOW TO STOP LEAKS IN YOUR POWER

Silence is an aid to concentrating Attention and energy.

You have a plan to which you have devoted much attention and about which you have adopted a definite and positive attitude. To put this plan into successful execution, you must depend upon your entire physical and mental energy. You can spare none of it and hope to achieve success. You are in the position of an engineer who must drive their locomotive a certain distance in a certain time on a known amount of diesel or electrical force.

You have the force within you already generated. Your machine is ready to start. You are headed in the proper direction, and you know the distance to be traveled.

But you want the world to know all about the great things you are going to do. So, you waste a few pounds of steam or volts of electricity in making a big noise about it. You advertise your intentions and attract prospective customers — but have nothing to show them, except a waste of energy.

Remember the predicament of the old riverboat captain with a small vessel and a big whistle. The whistle was so big the he had to stop the boat every time he blew it, because it took so much of his motive power! He didn't win any races, although he was the noisiest person on the Mississippi.

When you waste energy you have just that much less for purposeful work. Wasted energy cannot be recalled and concentrated by any amount of effort. You have to generate more energy.

You may be possessed of a superabundance of energy, such that you feel justified in diverting a good deal of it to the accomplishment of useless projects — but you may often wonder, in the event you fail of a much desired purpose, "what might have happened had I used my full force"?

But self-conscious waste of energy is something we can easily guard ourselves against. Where most of us fail in life, for lack of energy, is in being ignorant of the tremendous waste of our forces due to leaks in our mechanism. Until we find the leaks and stop them up, our full force cannot be concentrated on our work or anything else.

HOW ENERGY IS WASTED

Some of the more common leaks are:

1. Division of Attention between the task at hand and other things wholly unconnected with it. Review Lesson 1. This leak may be stopped by **SILENCE**, because in silence we can best withdraw our diffused attention from those things unrelated to the work at hand.

2. Indecision, vacillation, hesitation, otherwise known as "difficulty in making up our mind." Each time you "change your mind" about a plan of action you lose headway, which means you have wasted energy It is an indication that you have not thoroughly done the preliminary thinking and Planning before deciding to act. You have not exercised the necessary care in building the foundation from which to start your business structure. There is something wrong with your mental attitude; your degree of attention to the work at hand. It is important that you act only after making a definite decision which you are confident is a correct one. **ONCE ENTERED UPON A COURSE OF ACTION GO THROUGH WITH IT WITH ALL THE ENERGY AT YOUR COMMAND**. The "Quitter" never succeeds in business. They merely waste energy.

3. Destructive habits of thought and action. These are energy wasters of the worst type. They include wrong mental attitudes (see Lesson 2) and violations of the natural laws of mental and physical health As there are numerous text books advising one how best to maintain **HEALTH**, further comment upon the subject here is unnecessary, save to say that "bad habits" are like holes rusted in a water pipe. The stream of water is partially wasted through the tiny leaks and the pressure reduced where it is most needed.

4. Emotionalism, or failure to control one's emotions whether "good" or "bad." This source of energy waste is perhaps the most prolific source of business failure in the world. As in the case of destructive habits of thought and action, Emotionalism has the effect of drawing off energy through innumerable tiny leaks. These leaks are best stopped up with silence. That is we may learn to control our emotions more easily by keeping them to ourselves. It is a fact that an emotional person seems to derive pleasure in telling their friends all about the riot of emotions which produce the greatest trouble. And the infliction of the tale on others who probably have plenty of troubles of their own, emotional and otherwise, apparently has the effect of convincing: the teller they need makes no further effort to control themselves — that their long-suffering friends have in some manner relieved this person of the burden by listening to them. (See Lesson 6.)

Lack of Self-control always means loss of one's directing power over their own energy — consequently an opportunity for energy to leak out of any convenient channel of escape.

Such leaks of energy as just mentioned are best given the Silent treatment. Nature has provided the hours of sleep for recharging the body with energy — a sufficient proof that Nature demands Silence for the most efficient results.

So, when you are making your business plans that demand all your attention and energy; when you are most carefully considering the attitude you should establish — you will find that far less mental effort is required when you are closeted in a quiet place.

And when you are ready to act, don't talk about what you are going to do, but **DO IT** and others will do all the talking necessary. After you have done, the thing is time enough to talk — if at all — and then you will find that talk is unnecessary – the deed speaks for itself. Others will advertise it for you far better than you can.

SILENCE IS NOT ONLY A CONSERVATOR OF ENERGY — IT ATTRACTS ENERGY.

HOW TO SAVE ENERGY

Take a lesson from Nature's method of recharging an exhausted human body with energy. During the hours we are awake, every physical movement, every sensation, every thought, uses up some of our energy. During the natural silence of sleep, all the avenues of escape are closed to energy, which is constantly being generated in us from the food we eat, the air we breathe, and the water we drink.

As a consequence, our bodies are recharged in from four to eight hours, and we wake from a sound sleep full of vigor. Obviously, we require a definite amount of sleep in which to permit Nature to do this work, the time depending upon how we expend this stored up energy during the wakeful hours.

When an individual becomes familiar with their own mechanism, and observes how Nature uses Silence in keeping it constantly recharged with energy, they can aid Nature considerably and lessen her task by using the same methods. That is to say, they can consciously recharge themselves with energy during their wakeful hours so as to get along with far less sleep than Nature would otherwise demand.

To do this, one merely has to stop up the leaks of their energy by resorting to restful silence where they can more easily withdraw their attention from distracting sights, sounds and sensory impressions — all of which demand energy. These channels of energy being closed, Nature continues to manufacture energy within a person and to pour it into them from the outside as in sleep. As less energy is being used than is manufactured, naturally the body becomes recharged more quickly though not as quickly as in sleep.

THE MIND NEVER SLEEPS

Some sleep is absolutely essential for physiological reasons it is unnecessary to speak of here. The mind itself never goes to sleep — only the body. In perfect, natural sleep the mind is not using the physical body at all, for which reason Nature does her work more quickly. As long as we are awake, the mind must use the body to some extent, so that the silent rest of wakefulness requires somewhat longer than the silence and restfulness of sleep to thoroughly recharge the body with energy.

The tired business person will find that a good massage of their whole relaxed body after a refreshing bath, will also go far toward helping Nature recharge them with energy, because the massage does what the physical body does for itself during sleep — it squeezes out the waste products that clog the nerves and muscles and blood and allows new energy to flow freely.

CONTACTING THE UNIVERSAL SUPPLY

In Lesson 3 on Energy, we alluded to the fact that energy radiates from the body and that this radiating energy, being charged with our own thought impulses, creates a "Personal Atmosphere" around us which is subconsciously sensed by others with whom we come in contact.

We also learned that human vitality is drawn from food, drink and the atmosphere of the earth; that the human body is a huge converter of the lower life energies of plant, mineral, and animal into the higher energies of humanity.

These observations would lead us to suspect that Humanity is either the possessor of the highest form of energy in Nature, or that its own energies may be utilized and converted in some fashion into still higher forms. That is, if there is any purpose whatever in Nature, Humanity is the achievement of that purpose or else is merely a part of it.

Human energy drawn from minerals, plant, and animal, is not the highest form of energy. There is yet another force humanity can draw into itself and use, that for want of a better name has been called "Primary" or "Planetary" or "Universal" Energy. When so utilized, it becomes a part of our "personal magnetism" and has the effect of stimulating all our other energies.

What it is, we do not know, except for its effects.

It may be from the Sun or some other source of power, but it is certainly one of the most powerful forces human beings can attach to their machinery. It sweeps around the earth and through the earth and everything on it, in currents of force differing in velocity and power according to the nature of the resistance it meets. Some of these we recognize as telluric currents — the earth's magnetism flowing north and south between the poles — and the earth's electric currents flowing at right angles from east to west.

But there is another "flow" at right angles to these — A flow from "above." It passes through us constantly, without effects that we are aware of — until we interpose our **WILL** in its path and give it our **ATTENTION**. Then it invigorates us, and we are in touch with an inexhaustible supply of energy far more powerful, as a renovator of jaded body and spirit than the most powerful high frequency electric current.

Why this is so we do not know. It is simply so.

To contact this reservoir of Primary Energy, picture mentally its flow downward through you to the earth; then **WILL** it to recharge your body.

Unbelievable as it may be, the result will demonstrate the truth of the statement that when you turn your whole Attention to this source of energy, thereby withdrawing it from other things and producing the effect of "Silence" in stopping up the leaks of your personal energy supply, and simply **WILL** to hold enough of this stream of primary power — you become filled with it almost immediately.

It is as though your body were a vessel the bottom of which was made of movable flat plates swinging on hinges that allowed them to hang downward, perpendicular with the earth. A stream of water poured into the vessel would pass through without stopping. But when the flat plates are suddenly swung on their hinges parallel to the earth's surface so as to form a solid bottom, they resist the flow and the vessel quickly fills to the brim.

You may not succeed in this experiment at the first two or three trials. It is so simple and amazing that most people entirely ignorant of this little known source of energy, are inclined to ridicule rather than investigate. But the energy is there to be used by anyone who cares to do so.

AN EXPERIMENT

Try this, if you are skeptical:

Stand erect, relaxed in mind and body.

Stretch out your hands and arms at right angles to the body, palms up and keep in that position for about two minutes. You will feel a faint tingling in the palms, largely due perhaps to the withdrawal of blood from the hands and arms. After a brief rest, resume your position, but turn one palm down, horizontal to the earth's surface. The tingling will be more pronounced in the upturned palm and a little later in the down turned palm.

It is believed that here you are able to feel very faintly the physical reaction of the "Primary Energy" on the nerves of the palms, made especially sensitive because of the withdrawal of blood and the tension produced by the two-minute stretch of the arms. Do not tire yourself. It is inadvisable to stretch out your arms more than two minutes at a time.

Now in addition to holding the position suggested, (whether you have any faith in the experiment or not), let your whole mental attitude toward it be such as though you accepted it as a working theory for the moment, and **WISH** strongly (i.e. Will it to be so) that the stream of down flowing energy fill you completely. You should be able to feel a warmth first in your upturned palm, then filling your whole body by spreading out from your solar plexus and then flowing out the down turned palm.

The experiment is suggested merely for purpose of demonstration. It is not at all necessary to assume any particular position to stop the current — i.e. "contact" it. It is a Natural force and needs but the power of human will thrust in its stream to "contact it" and utilize its power, just as an engineer uses a hydroelectric dam to "contact" a stream of water by interposing a turbine in its course. If we have leaky minds and bodies, we will not be able to use or hold much of the stream. If our machinery is in good condition, we can hold and use what we will.

The practical object of utilizing this outside store of energy, which comes to us best in Silence, is to supplement the normal supply derived from food so as to make it possible to answer the extraordinary demands upon our personal energy made by modern civilization. This energy does not take the place of energy drawn from food, drink or the air we breathe, though it supplements them all — it makes them last longer.

The life elements of food taken into the body are already partially manufactured products of this same primary energy especially adapted to human use. They are, as it were, but concentrated primary energy — yet of a consistency required by the grosser parts of our being, whereas the primary energy can only act as a stimulant, because it is not concentrated as a physical "food."

PRACTICE THE FOLLOWING EXERCISE DAILY

Silence — Take ten minutes each day, at any time during your work or play hours, lock yourself up in a quiet place and absolutely relax yourself in mind and body. Either sit or lie in a comfortable position. Do not think of any particular thing — that is, let your Attention be free to dwell upon whatever it will. A very good position of relaxation when sitting is to let the hands lie palm up in the lap, or, when lying, to fold them behind your head.

When relaxed in this manner, note carefully what thoughts arise in your mind and fasten your attention upon the first pleasant one; examine it; note what association of ideas it arouses; if there are unpleasant ones, reject them and give attention only to the pleasant ones. This is "daydreaming" if you will — but important, since it has for its purpose, pleasurable emotion, and emotion being power, you are storing up the right sort of emotion by focusing attention (and therefore focusing energy).

This little period of silence may be utilized in various ways. The method may be varied. But always take the ten minutes or longer if you can afford it.

Thus, you may take into your room a thing of beauty — A rose for example; a picture; a good book. Relax first — then, instead of waiting for thoughts, let your attention dwell upon the rose, the picture or the book.

Or, if you are pressed for time, you can "kill two birds with one stone" by making a note during the day of the most perplexing business problem you have and taking that into your silent chamber instead of a book. But relax first and remain physically relaxed. Mentally your attention is given to the problem stated briefly on your paper. Do not attempt to solve it so much as to examine it attentively — note what association of ideas it arouses. Be passive rather than active mentally. Be mentally receptive to the ideas that come in connection with the problem. If you distrust your memory, jot them down on paper to be thought over actively afterward.

Do this daily, and you will learn the value of silence better than any words can describe it.

7

LESSON V

VISION

Without mental vision — the power to "think ahead" — mentally to project oneself into the future and prepare oneself to meet possible future conditions in ones business, no worker can successfully compete with others who are able to do these things.

Everyone has the power of Vision, though not all possess it equally, since we are all in different stages of evolution mentally. Nor does everyone cultivate this latent power. Everyone can and should do so.

By reference to your dictionary, you will find that the word Vision has its roots in old Greek and Latin words meaning "to see," and "to know," while going back still further, it is akin to words meaning **"IDEAS."**

Next, we find that we Visualize an Idea so that we obtain a good mental picture of it as an object or a symbol or a combination of both, by an effort of what is known as **"IMAGINATION"** that is our "image making faculty." It is often called our "Creative" faculty. By it we actually create mental pictures and artistic designs.

We "See" these imaginary pictures "in our minds" and by focusing our Attention upon them, often arrive at definite convictions about them which seem to us, if not to others, to be almost if not quite, actual **KNOWLEDGE**. Young children have the power of visualizing ideas in this way so clearly, that they often frighten themselves by the vividness of their imaginations. They often "see" the imaginary picture objectively, and it is as real to them as a tree or a horse is to our objective sight. In

48

such wise they "create" a world all of their own and live in it with as much enjoyment as we do in the objective world.

IMAGINATION – A POWER

Perhaps because we "grew up" folks, have for ages accustomed ourselves to dismiss "Imagination" as childish, and therefore of no consequence, most of us overlook the fact that Imagination is the most vital thing in Vision — the foundation upon which visions are built. It is the one "Creative" faculty of the soul.

Yet there must be some substantial reason for Imagination because individuals of Vision have always been wonderfully successful in this world when they had all the other qualifications of success. Nations governed by individuals of vision have endured long after those nations lacking in such remarkable people have disappeared.

Even science has been often retarded by lack of vision. When some scientist of real vision solves a problem or invents an aid to human progress, as a rule they are first unreasonably ridiculed by their fellows academicians then rationally doubted, then logically approved and finally acclaimed one of the great ones. Virtually every step forward taken by humanity has been the result of someone's vision. The vision of Elijah's chariot was but a mental picture of our modern airplane.

So it is with business. People with "original ideas", of "initiative", of "foresight" are those who do the big work of the world or cause it to be done.

Now since Vision is literally a projection of intelligence into the future, it is essential for us to know just **HOW** this projection is achieved.

We judge future events by past experience, because past experience has taught us to know that everything that happens must have a definite cause, and that cause and effect are the result of some natural law. Nothing happens by "chance. There is no such thing as "luck" as being something without cause. If we understand the exact law that produces the cause, we can with confidence predict the effect, even though we do not know and cannot predict what change human will may make in it.

Humankind is of very finite intelligence and by experience knows only what will probably happen under any given set of circumstances. This is because humanity cannot say with assurance that it **"KNOWS"** all about the operation of any natural law. Its knowledge is only relative — not absolute.

"LOOKING AHEAD"

But when we observe the same thing happen in the same way and under the same circumstances every time those circumstances manifest, we feel justified in the conclusion that we have "discovered" the law involved. And so, we feel further justified in holding that if the same act or circumstances prevail at any future time they will be followed by the same effects produced in the past.

For this reason, history, the arts and sciences, and all other records of human experience are valuable to the business person. They are aids to Vision. They are the database of all visions of the future. For human Vision is but the reflection of the past in the mirror of the future.

You are a living history of your own experience and the experience of all your ancestors to a certain extent. The "written record" of this history is contained in that which you call your "Memory," a subject to be dealt with in Lesson 7.

Now if one is able to dig down into their memory and bring up past experiences recorded there, that will either — exactly or even approximately fit a certain combination of circumstances that an individual has reason to believe will exist at a future period — that person may with some confidence and certainty predict the result.

Further, since the records of memory are those of actual occurrences — that is, of actual experience — they constitute a certain store of knowledge. Predictions based upon knowledge naturally have the weight of authority.

To illustrate: The predictions and forecasts of the business market by expert statisticians often seem as remarkable as the utterances of the ancient prophets because they have for decades observed and tabulated cause and effect in their special fields of research. The charted results reveal to them something approximating a "law" that governs these causes and effects. By fitting past experience to present and future conditions they predict future results with remarkable accuracy.

Life insurance experience tables are an example of the reliance business people place upon such statistics. The number of successful insurance companies conducted in accord with these tables (now representing about 200 years of experience) is a demonstration of their value. From such statistical records, the business person feels reasonably safe in doing business by what they call the "law of averages."

This sort of business vision is now in such common use that many moderately successful business people prefer to conduct their business by the set rules and statistical tables drawn up by others, rather than risk their own powers of observation and reason. Of course these people are not themselves possessed of either courage or vision — but they are at least sensible enough to recognize the value of vision in others.

As Vision is founded on the science of mental "image making"— **IMAGINATION** — The first thing to do is to exercise and make stronger this wonderful faculty. Do not be afraid of your imagination. It is a real working tool. Your statistician used their imagination to picture all those mountain ranges of figures on the little charts which financiers, bankers, manufacturers, and executives of all sorts use so confidently. Their pictures were "imagined" from facts — and so they are true.

AN EXPERIMENT

Try on yourself a little experiment in Imagination.

I utter the word "Apple."

Immediately your imagination pictures to your mental eye the form of an Apple — red, russet, yellow perhaps. That picture was in your Memory. Imagination simply got it out and used it, painted it to suit your taste and held it before your Attention. I bet some of you thought of the company and its products, but no a plain old juicy apple was what I was proposing for this experiment.

But I tell you I had a **GREEN** apple in mind and not red, russet or yellow. Instantly Imagination paints your apple green.

So you see Imagination is the foundation of vision because it enables you to "visualize" mentally, any stated set of facts or conditions within your own experience or observation. Just how imagination does this is of no consequence here and is to be discussed elsewhere. But imagination does it.

From the materials stored in your memory, your mind can build whatever picture it desires. And it is by building pictures that your mind can peer a little way into the future of the business world. Otherwise the business person must remain as blind as a bat to the future of their business. Even were someone else gifted with the power to see where that person could not, that other could not make themselves comprehended by the business person if the mental pictures are not there for Imagination to use. We cannot understand that which passes the powers of Imagination.

The individual who uses Vision is like the mechanic who searches through their odds and ends of material to find a screw that will fit a particular hole. To use Imagination in creating Vision for business purposes, the Will must make proper choice of the experience pictures brought up from memory by imagination.

The more you use Imagination the greater becomes your store of mental images — that is the greater your store of experience becomes, since every picture represents an experience. It is by Imagination that you improve Memory as you will note in Lesson 7.

Bear in mind that while exercising your Imagination you have a definite set of purposes in view:

A. To find a set of experience pictures that will fit your particular set of circumstances which have given rise to the problem you wish to solve.

B. To give your Attention only to those pictures and trains of thought which spring from them, that seem to be related to your problem.

C. By this process of elimination, you will arrive at consideration of but two or three such picture groups.

D. After careful consideration and reasoning and perhaps seeking the advice of others, you will select one set of pictures and make it your plan of action.

E. You have then only to translate thought into action.

All builders of business use Vision. The architect must Imagine their plans before putting them on paper; the inventor, the thing they want to invent before making a model of it. The peddler of shoe strings looks forward with their Imagination to a shoe store; the storekeeper to a factory; the factory owner to a combination of factories where efficiency and economy will mean greater Service translated into more Money. These individuals of vision who know how to translate Vision into reality seem to have no limitations in achievement.

It will pay the business person handsomely to build themselves a vision of their Business as an exchange of Service.

PRACTICE THE FOLLOWING EXERCISE DAILY

Vision — Daily take five or ten minutes at any time you choose (at night before retiring or in the morning before getting out of bed are good times) and in Silence contemplate your own purpose in business. Select what you are sure is your greatest Purpose. Focus Attention upon that and note carefully all the thoughts and chains of ideas that seem to well up in your mind in connection with this purpose.

Continually ask yourself as each of these mental pictures forms, **COULD IT BE BETTER AND BIGGER? HOW?**

Just that, nothing more.

And as you ask these questions, Imagination gets more and more active, presenting you mental structures beyond anything you have, perhaps, ever before thought of.

This, too, is "day-dreaming," and may even be carried over into real dreams during sleep but it is important because it is **VISION** presenting to you patterns that have been worked out by Sub-consciousness for you to build from.

Therefore: — I am a plodder. I've always worked for a salary which is inadequate to supply my desires. In these periods of visioning, Imagination has pictured structures of considerable grandeur, placing me amid desirable conditions wherein my income kept pace with my needs for comfort and happiness. "Castles in Spain?" Yes.

But something more — for there is that question, **"HOW?"**

As a plodder, Vision tells me I remain so because I do not **KNOW** enough to be anything else. What else am I fit for? What else can I do except plod? Can I learn other things? Why not? Others have done so. There are correspondence schools, night classes, public night schools, Internet courses — all anxious to teach me.

What if I gave some of my time, energy and attention to one of these? I see in my visions how I may keep at my work in which I have become a plodder and work myself out of plodding into things that will earn me more income. I act upon the vision and soon go up and out of plodding. Many people have doubled their income the first year. Many are now in their original positions — but no longer plodding; they are, perhaps, doing other things to add to their income. Some do half a dozen.

VISION POINTS A WAY. CULTIVATE IT DAILY.

8

LESSON VI

EMOTION

Emotion is powerful.

Control of emotion means control of power.

Never attempt to destroy or permanently suppress an emotion; for in so doing you are inviting self-destruction.

By reference to your dictionary, you will discover that "Emotions" are the "movers out" of the mind.

All sights, sounds, odors, tastes and "feelings" arouse what are called "emotions." You are conscious of a response within you to their stimuli — a vague disturbance of some sort you are generally unable to define precisely.

Your "pity" is aroused by distressing sights.

You become "angry" when someone or something affronts you.

Your "sense of humor" is touched by one thing and your "sense of honor" by another. You "love" or "hate," or experience "hunger," "fear," "thirst," "desire" — because of these inner responses to sensory impressions.

Many people are often called "courageous" when they are simply ignorant of the danger we should naturally expect them to "fear." We say "they have no nerves" — or that they have "nerves of steel."

Upon careful analysis we find that all the sensory impressions which arouse "Emotion," reach our inner world of consciousness through the medium of one or more of the so-called "senses" — hearing, feeling, seeing, etc.; and that they are invariably accompanied by an inner response that brings up from Memory some thought, some mental picture, that is the counterpart of the message from outside.

This thought — (which we call a "memory") — represents some real or imaginary experience of our own. It is a sympathetic bond between the inner and the outer worlds — and we name it "an emotion." One is but the reflection of the other. The response is the effect; the impression the cause. We feel these effects by means of the "sympathetic nerve system" which comes to a center in the solar plexus. Different individuals feel them in slightly different ways, according to how sensitive their sympathetic nerves are to the sensory impulse felt. The nerves become more sensitive through right use.

KNOWLEDGE GAINED THROUGH SENSE

From all this you will note that we acquire all our material for knowledge first, through the sympathetic nerve system which is the nerve system of latent or "sub-consciousness." That is to say, we see, feel, hear, taste, or smell things by distinguishing the vibrations of energy which give rise to sight, feeling, hearing, tasting or smelling, through the specially adapted nerves of sense which receive and respond to those vibrations only.

After the impression has been made on our nerves of sense and responded to, we can reason about it and learn just what it is, how and why it affects us. That is, we can focus our attention upon the experience and analyze it to obtain a knowledge of it.

Or as is most frequently the case, we can ignore it by refusing it our attention, so that the experience will remain in subconsciousness (latent consciousness) indefinitely without our being aware of it until it is aroused by some other emotion and presents itself suddenly before us to our considerable astonishment and mystification.

EVERY EMOTION, THEREFORE, IS POTENTIAL
KNOWLEDGE AND KNOWLEDGE IS POWER

When emotions are ignored or suppressed, we remain ignorant of their character, meaning and power — but we neither "forget" them nor "destroy" them. They still have the power of "moving out" (Emotion) the mind, and will almost invariably do so when we personally least expect it.

Hence, it is important to know all about our emotions. We should study them carefully in order to control them.

For example, we should consider everything that has the ability to make us "angry" so that we "lose our temper" — (i.e. our Self-control) in order that we may be ready in an instant's notice to assert our mastery over the emotion, "anger," in case it "moves out" with some sudden explosion and controls us. Just why does a certain person, or an argument, or an injustice arouse our anger? And when anger is aroused, do we "subconsciously" feed it by brooding over all the similar occurrences that have produced this same emotion in the past? And why?

To permit anger to sweep aside our common sense is bad for business. That much we instinctively know. And so we know that when any emotion whatever is permitted to dominate us instead of being dominated by us, it is a weakness of which an enemy or a rival may take advantage to our hurt. But we also instinctively realize that these same emotions, if brought under control of our own Will, are forces that may be used either offensively or defensively.

HOW TO CHECK EMOTION

We may check the outward spread of an emotion from its point of origin merely by focusing our Attention upon it — which, in the language of the street, is to "look before you leap" — to "think twice before you speak," to "look yourself in the face" and "use your head."

Then, while Attention grasps the emotion by the neck as it were, holding it momentarily captive, a determined effort of the Will, in a twinkling can twist or push it into a change of Attitudes — that is a change of direction, if needed. Your emotion then has lost none of its impetus — no power or energy is wasted — but it has been given definite and constructive direction. Or, as some writers put it, the emotion has been "converted," or "transformed," or "transmuted."

OVERCOMING FEAR

To illustrate:

"Fear" is one of those "movers out of the mind," which, uncontrolled, sometimes kills its victim and at all times destroys confidence in oneself. It is a freezing process, in which the nerves and whole body seem to congeal. It seems to start with a wave of numbness that spreads quickly outward from the solar plexus. Complete fear is very rare, but every business person in the world probably knows some of the symptoms after a brief "battle" with a money panic that threatens the extinction of their business or that menaces their loved ones as well as themselves with poverty.

This person knows that if this feeling is allowed to go unchecked within them, it will quickly incapacitate them for work, or even for effective thinking. A real person reacts to the feeling of fear almost automatically — that is, "sub-consciously." They will put up some kind of fight against it in order that other people may think they "game," because they know the business world has little use for a coward. In such cases it is fear of ridicule and contempt that overpowers fear of failure!

But the "Fear" is merely given slightly new direction — a more constructive direction it is true. Yet some of the Fear remains active, with a tendency to return to its original direction because it is not held in check intelligently and self-consciously. Practically the only resistance the original "fear of failure" meets with, is a sub-conscious "fear of contempt"— "afraid of being afraid." The second is an emotion aroused by the first — and being a secondary emotion, is weaker than the original, until, involuntarily, Attention is drawn to it and away from the "fear of failure," thereby opening a wider and wider channel for the force of both "fears" to flow through.

Eventually, it may be, almost the entire force of the original "fear" is flowing through this new channel — this new conductor of energy provided wholly, or in part, by "sub-conscious" processes. Therefore, Nature has endowed the individual with an automatic resistance to the destructive action of their own emotions.

Nature, however, can do no more than this without the individual's aid. Unless they make an effort **THEMSELVES** — that is unless they assert their Self-conscious powers and interposes their Will to resist the destructive action of emotion, such destructive action will continue to spread outward from its point of origin in obedience to the same natural law that causes the concentric waves of water to spread from a stone splashed in the middle of a pond.

It is because "Sub-consciousness" is in the process of being "Self defined" in individuals, that it offers some resistance to the "waves of emotionalism." Sub-consciousness forces its way even to the Attention of Self-consciousness with its warnings to resist fear.

It is at this point where Self-conscious Attention is momentarily compelled to "listen" to the inner warning against unbridled emotion, that Humanity may freely and voluntarily seize the Emotion by the "scruff of its neck," with its Self-conscious Attention and hold it there under the scrutiny of Reason, long enough to decide its new direction (Attitude) — and give it a deliberate push in that direction.

To sum up the effects, we discover that Fear can be turned into an impulse toward safety, or it can be stopped and turned right about face in order to fight the conditions "feared," whereupon it becomes "Courage." So, "Hate" can be diverted into altruistic channels or even "changed" into "Love"; pessimism can be transmuted into optimism; anger into tolerance and even pleasure.

Every Emotion may be diverted into channels of constructive action when it originates as a destructive agency and may also be "converted" into its exact opposite, without losing any of its force; all by the simple application of the principles of Attention and Attitude.

Conversely, all emotions that originate constructively, may be deliberately turned into destructive channels — though no sane person will therefore deliberately attempt suicide.

BUSINESS PEOPLE SHOULD STUDY EMOTION

To the business person, the subject of Emotion is one of the most important to which they could possibly turn their Attention. Not only their own Emotions but those of other people with whom they have or may have business dealings with, are factors that, at any time, may determine the success or failure of those dealings.

All successful business people are "readers of character" in others. They know the emotional weakness or strength of those with whom they do business. Self-protection should impel them to know their own strength and weakness in this respect.

Our emotional life is the natural consequence of experience for without experience we could have no emotion. It is doubtful if there could be such a thing as human personality, without emotion. Hence, we must deal with emotion as a distinctively human attribute as well as a definite power. (animal emotion is almost wholly beyond the control of the animal as an entity — that is, animals are not capable of Self-control.)

Emotions are capable of classification as are the various forms of energy such as steam, electricity, radio-rays, winds, tides, etc. Each emotion has its definite use as a starter of mental activity, analogous to the action of a spark-plug of an automobile, whose flash starts the whole machinery.

It would be interesting, from a scientific standpoint, to consider the precise action of every emotion on the glands that secrete those juices freighted with various forms of stored up energy that are used by the body to accomplish work. But that is unnecessary here, because this is a book for business people and not for scientists.

Yet, every business person has had (or should have) an understanding of some of the things science has discovered about each of us, since the subject of glands and the renewal of vigor through the transplantation of glands has become of exceeding interest to worn out business people.

ABOUT YOUR GLANDS AND EMOTIONS

Briefly, you have a system of nerves divided into two sub-systems, one of them known as the "Sympathetic" system which connects and centralizes the so-called "Sub-conscious" or "involuntary" processes, and the other the "Cerebrospinal" or "Voluntary" system which connects and centralizes the so-called self-conscious processes.

The Solar Plexus or big nerve ganglia over the stomach is the central brain of the Sympathetic system. The "Brain" or mass of nerve cells in the head is the central brain of the Cerebrospinal system and the seat of human personality. Each system has a number of sub-brains scattered at various points along the main trunk line of its nerves — the Pneumogastric Nerve in the Sympathetic system and the Spinal Cord in the Cerebrospinal System.

In these "brains" is stored away your energy which is in active use. Energy which is not in active use — that is our surplus energy — is stored away in a number of glands. Each of these glands is located within or near one of the various "brains" or nerve centers and is surrounded by webs of nerves and blood vessels which pour their surplus energies into the glands.

Each gland secretes a juice which is filled with minute particles of matter that serve as storage batteries of energy, so that we may regard the gland as filled with "liquid energy" in such form that when there is some pressure on the gland, the juice it contains is discharged and its tiny storage batteries by the millions, contained in the juices, hasten to discharge their energies into whatever part of the body calls for them.

Obviously it is important to keep our physical machinery of blood, nerves and glands in good working order. Nature will do this for us if we obey natural rules of health.

Now, an emotion is primarily, and from a physical and chemical point of view, a readjustment of energy conditions in the nerve cells. There is a discharge of energy in one cell, necessitating its being recharged from the next cell and so on, until the central brain is reached, when a reflex action begins.

You cannot move a finger, or breathe or think without setting up one of these general waves of emotional discharge of energy. It is clear, therefore, that all human movement, including thought, burns up energy. We cannot use energy without depleting to some extent the supply of the "brain" affected.

We cannot deplete this supply without that particular "brain" seeking to recharge itself from its special storehouse — a gland. For, therein is its reserve store of energy. So, we see that Emotion is one of the commonest and most necessary things in life and that its action is automatic and sub-conscious, until we focus attention upon it.

Fits of Emotionalism, more common in some and uncommon in others, perhaps, leave the victim physically and mentally exhausted, first, because they fail to check emotion with their Attention and second, because they allow it to pursue whatever path it chooses, by failing to determine its Attitude themselves. In other words, the victim permits the emotion to control their entire being to whatever extent they fail to assert Self-mastery.

As a consequence of this physical and mental exhaustion, when Emotion is permitted to control, the victim must store up more energy before they can regain their normal powers. An engineer who would deliberately waste steam or electrical power, in this way would at once loose their job. But the person who wastes their own energy (by giving way to emotionalism) cannot very well discharge themselves. They can only make up their mind to learn Self-control.

PROOF THAT WILL IS POSITIVE

Uncontrolled emotion is the strongest possible physical evidence that human energy is receptive to Will power; that Will is the positive and controlling factor in deciding a person's destiny. Emotion is primarily a "sub-conscious" process and therefore an automatic mental process. To control it with Will is to make it a Self-conscious and therefore, a personal mental process. Never be deceived by those who would have you believe that humanity is helpless against "Sub-consciousness."

Since Emotion is a "mover out of the mind," we are justified in asking just **WHAT** it does "move out"— for "the mind" includes a lot of things in its mechanism.

The answer is, that Emotion, first of all, sets in motion the energy currents of the body which cause the repetition of physical reactions that produce "Memories."

Memories create desires.

Uncontrolled emotion piles up these memories and desires in the greatest confusion. Then our normal mental equilibrium is upset.

We Self-consciously reason the way out — climb to the top of this rubbish heap and assert our personal independence of it. **BUT WHERE IS THE TOP OR BOTTOM?**

Because we have lost self-control when emotion is "running wild," there are so many confusing things whirling around us we have lost our sense of direction and even of location. **OUR ATTITUDE IS UNKNOWN. OUR ATTENTION IS UTTERLY DISPERSED.**

Yet we can quickly **THINK** ourselves free of this dilemma.

HOW TO BE FREE OF EMOTIONALISM

We have only to seize the first emotion or part of an emotion that presents itself most strongly to what powers of Attention may be left to us, hold to it and "pull ourselves together" as the saying is. Upon captive emotion, "Will" concentrates the force of Attention that attains greater and greater focus the longer we "concentrate."

Once having brought Attention to a focus on one part of the emotional chaos, we are in position to apply the principle of Attitude and change its direction toward constructive channels. One by one we go through that rubbish heap of emotions with Attention and Attitude and presently find ourselves again Masters, with Emotion brought under control of Will.

SELF CONTROL

No successful business person in the world wants to employ or work with another who has no power of Self-control.

Loss of self-control is not only a psychological crime but a business crime, because it means loss of energy and efficiency. It means loss of the sense of responsibility. The uncontrolled individual cannot be successful in business.

The only useful place in life they can fill is that of a worker under direction of the Self-controlled individual. Otherwise, they are energy wasters, time wasters and hindrances to business or any other sort of human progress.

If you have not the ability to control yourself at all times, your problem is clearly defined. It is to discover the leaks of energy and the kinds of energy connected with your periodic outbreaks of emotionalism. Stop the leaks by refusing to surrender or throw away your Self-control. Concentrate your Attention on retaining the **POWER** of your emotions by changing their Attitude.

AS TO "AUTO-SUGGESTION"

In conclusion, a word on so-called "Auto-suggestion" may not be amiss, as it is a subject now in vogue with lecturers on "Applied Psychology" — and also is a very easily misconstrued word.

At the beginning of the 20th century (spring of 1922) a Monsieur Emile Coue of Nancy, France, created quite a furor in England by his lectures on Auto-suggestion and Self-mastery, in which he attempted to explain how mind may conquer even certain physical ills of the body through correct thinking.

Where many laypeople, unaccustomed to scientific terms, become confused concerning such advice, is in supposing that "Auto-suggestion" is synonymous with "Self-hypnotism." There is no such thing as the latter because it is impossible for "Hypnotism" to exist unless one mind exercises control over another. It is true that certain psychologists used to suppose that we had **TWO MINDS** — one the "Subliminal" or "Subconscious" and the other the "Conscious" — by which they meant the "Self-conscious" part of our being. But science long ago abandoned this absurdity, which Monsieur Coue tried to revive. His account of "Auto-suggestion" is full of fact but confused as to terminology, as when he uses the words "Will" and "Imagination" in misleading ways, often the reverse of what is true.

Each of us is only **ONE** person. Self-consciousness is completely individualized intelligence and Sub-consciousness is incompletely individualized self. If both of these parts of the one human mind were separate minds — that is separate individualities or persons, then it would be proper to say that John Smith was also Sam Jones and that Smith could hypnotize Jones or vice versa.

While all this may seem like splitting hairs to the average non-scientific business person, it is very important for them to know if they intend to utilize their powers of "Auto-suggestion" in their business affairs. Otherwise, they will become confused between processes that may lead them into mental dangers when they seek to apply "suggestion" to others and find themselves doing just the reverse — using hypnotism.

"Self" is **YOU**.

Self-consciousness has the power to suggest, even to demand of Sub-consciousness, as a parent to a child. Subconsciousness is the child, with mind unformed and incomplete in growth, compared to Self-consciousness.

Sub-consciousness exists for the sole purpose of obeying and ministering to the needs of Self-consciousness. It feeds Self-consciousness. Self-consciousness grows upon it. Sub-consciousness is the perfect servant. Self-consciousness, when exercising complete Self control is the perfect Master.

In this relation, "Auto-suggestion" (so-called) does accomplish astonishing results in Self-cure; in Memory; in changing one's mental and physical habits by changing Attitude. Constant command of Self to Sub-consciousness results in the latter establishing a definite Attitude (see Lesson 2) conforming to Will.

But the whole subject of Auto-suggestion can be demonstrated to be nothing more nor less than a phase of Self-control. So what has been said in this lesson as to Emotion, covers Auto-suggestion.

To illustrate the power of "Auto-suggestion" however, the following experiments are suggested:

1. Determine to wake up in the morning at a certain hour, or when a certain thing occurs, such as the arrival of the milkman; impressing upon your own mind the necessity of doing this. Result, you will wake up at the time stipulated.

2. You wish to remember to do a certain thing at a certain time. For instance, your wife asks you to mail a letter (What business person has not forgotten letters?) so it will get in the post office for the next train. You are to do this on your way downtown.

Before you leave home, note attentively where you put the letter and say to yourself as you put it there, "I will remember to mail this as I get off the car at Blank Street — or as I take my desk key from my pocket — or as I pass the big sign on Smith's store which I notice every morning." And you will remember as you have suggested.

3. You wish to break yourself of a bad habit — Say of scowling when you talk. You do not intend to be "grouchy" nor do you feel especially pessimistic. You know the scowl is a habit and that the cure for it is a smile. So — smile deliberately. After a while you will do it "without thinking." Your scowling habit will change to a smiling habit.

The sub-conscious reflexes of the mind have given rise to a world of philosophy and text books. But the important and outstanding fact for business people to know is, that when you self-consciously and with definite purpose determine to do a thing —or "set yourself a task"— you are giving orders that will be obeyed without question or reason, by the sub-conscious part of your mind.

When your whole self-conscious attention and attitude and energy are directed toward the accomplishment of a certain task, sub-consciousness follows without demur. It is the perfect and willing servant. It never thinks for itself but for you because it is not of that degree of intelligence that reasons. You must reason for it. When you order, it executes as you have ordered until you tell it to stop.

If you tell a sick stomach to get well, it will make a desperate effort to do so. It will build its Attitude and use its Energy just as you demand. But you have to be square with it by obeying Natural Law yourself. You can't think health into a stomach you continue to load down with all sorts of poisons and indigestible foods. It is what you actually demand of subconsciousness and not what you think should be demanded, that is obeyed. Subconsciousness is somewhat like an obedient child, of great intelligence.

And like a child, it is easily guided through emotional turmoil by a kind but firm parental mind. Like the child, it is constantly in action, full of energy — responding to everything it sees, hears, or otherwise "senses." The child bestows its energy in every direction and with few purposes in view. The parent turns the energy to good use.

PRACTICE THE FOLLOWING EXERCISE DAILY

Emotion — Arouse some of your pleasurable emotions each day. They are the easiest to control. Make it a habit to take a swim, play a game, see a picture show (a good one) or theater, or read a story each day. Whatever you do, endeavor to derive as much enjoyment from it as possible. Give particular attention to arousing the best of your emotions.

Nothing so arouses the emotions as to do a kind deed. If you have time for nothing else, adopt the custom of Marcus Aurelius never to let the setting sun go down without some good deed done. That is also the lesson many business people can take from the Scouts or the Guides!

Since Emotions are movers out of the mind, you naturally want the movement to be as pleasant as possible.

For the best results, do not talk much about your emotions. Simply arouse them, retain them within your own breast, and you will find them capable of augmenting your mental and physical energies; giving you new vigor, life and happiness. Emotion is Power. Control it.

Do this daily.

9

LESSON VII

MEMORY

Memory is the business person's library of information; their own mental filing system; their record of experience and observation; and their reference in all matters of doubt or difficulty.

The word "Memory" is very loosely used to describe both a mechanism and a process and also the thing produced by them! We say that an impression is "recorded in memory" or that "memory brings before us" visions of the past. Here we use the term to describe a mechanism or device for filing mental impressions or pictures.

When we refer to our "powers of memory" or set out to "memorize a thing," we allude to the mechanical action or power of action of our above-mentioned recording device.

But after the machine has been set in motion and its parts are working in perfect accord, we say that a "memory arises" or is "recalled." Here we are speaking of the manufactured article, as it were — the thing produced by the action (memory) of the machine (memory).

Hence in entering upon a study of their own "memory" and how to cultivate it, the business person may be somewhat at a loss to know exactly what their instructor is talking about, or, if they attempt to follow one of the many text-books upon "Memory," just what the author intends. A very large volume indeed could be written on the subject of "Memory" as the term is used by the average writer and speaker.

To the scientific psychologist, it is a most fascinating study to analyze the physical mechanism connected with memory; follow its operation during the period of chemical, electromagnetic, and mental reactions that take place within cells and organs of the body while a "Memory" is being aroused or put back into place and finally to classify the causes and effects produced.

MEMORY DEFINED

But for the benefit of the practical business person with little or no time to devote to the purely scientific phases of the subject, and yet with a desire to **USE** their memory to the greatest business advantage, it seems first of all important, to define Memory, then to set forth directions as to its use.

As the word is used in this lesson,

MEMORY IS THE MENTAL REPRODUCTION OF PAST EXPERIENCES SO AS TO BE RECOGNIZED, AS SUCH, BY THE ONE REPRODUCING THEM.

While this definition limits the meaning of **"MEMORY"** to those impressions on consciousness which we are able to recognize as records of our own past, (all other so-called memories, subconscious and otherwise being referred to other categories), it will enable the business person to note clearly the truth of the statement in Lesson 1, that,

"MEMORY IS BUT THE EVIDENCE OF THE DEGREE OF ATTENTION."

One will further note, as pointed out in Lesson 4 on Vision, that **MEMORY MAY BE DELIBERATELY SET IN MOTION BY IMAGINATION.**

In fact, it is always by exercising the image making faculty of the mind (Imagination) that the business person makes most effective use of memory.

WHAT CONSTITUTES EXPERIENCE

The mental records of past experiences are impressions made on consciousness by vibrating energy proceeding from the thing that makes the impression.

That is we experience the sensation of sight when light vibrations from the thing seen strike the nerve ends of the eye, which are specially adapted to detect them — and nothing else. Another set of special nerves in the ear detects sound vibrations and nothing else. The nerve ends on the tongue detect taste vibration; those in the nose vibrations of smell; those in the skin, a great variety of vibrations which we classify as those of "touch" or "feeling."

Each degree of vibration affects one of our senses, sets the special sense nerves to vibrating in harmony with it, flashes a message about what is happening to the center of perception directly connected with those nerves, and we say that we have seen, felt, tasted, smelt, heard or seen something; that is we have had an experience of that thing whether it be a material object or an idea.

Experience is **KNOWLEDGE**. Hence, it is obvious that we gain all the **KNOWLEDGE** we possess, through such experiences — through our sensory organism.

When we are able to recall at will these experiences, after they are past, we have a "memory" that is a most valuable business asset.

PENALTY OF FORGETTING

Unfortunately, few human beings, especially among business people and women, seem to possess more than mediocre ability to recall these experiences at will. They are first class "forgetters" and very poor "rememberers." Otherwise the business world would surely not repeat its mistakes so often and the great world of humanity would be happier.

There would be less poverty. There would be a more general recognition of the fact that business is an exchange of service for service.

For, humanity would remember that experience has repeatedly demonstrated that all attempts to evade the natural law of business have to be paid for, in the long run, with disastrous panics; that every attempt to force the natural law meets with disaster.

They would surely understand, if they remembered, that business ills can be permanently cured only by everyone giving an honest day's work for an honest day's pay and vice versa.

These things are all recorded in the minds of humanity. They simply receive little or no attention. And herein is the distinct cause of many a business or social calamity.

HOW WE GET A MEMORY

Consciousness is the prime factor in Memory.

Nature has established the following conditions in every normal human being for enabling them to remember impressions made on their general consciousness.

(a). Every cell of the human body is a conscious entity, made up of smaller conscious particles called molecules; these of still smaller bodies known as atoms; these of still finer divisions called electrons — Also "conscious," since they too respond to outside stimulation. Each finer division represents consciousness in some degree. Consciousness is always intelligent. General consciousness possesses a general intelligence and special consciousness a special intelligence, so it is to be noted that each of these divisions of cell matter represents a different stage or degree of intelligence. These degrees of intelligence are all working together in the cell under the centralized directing power of the cell — focused apparently in its nucleus or "brain."

(b). All energy and all matter (regarded as condensed energy) is necessarily intelligent and conscious in some degree. That outside the body is called "Universal Consciousness," sometimes "Cosmic Consciousness"— it is a general consciousness.

That inside the body is a collective consciousness of all its parts in the process of individualization or "self-definition" if we wish to coin a word that will fit the case. The cells coordinate their powers in groups, such as glands and organs and nerve systems.

These inner and outer worlds of intelligent consciousness are in constant contact through the medium of that radioactive phenomenon alluded to in Lesson 3 as the "Personal Atmosphere."

(c). Any stimulus from the outside, such as heat, light, a blow or any other form of vibration, is therefore bound to create an impression on human consciousness, provided it is within the receiving radius.

(d). Such physical stimuli as objects seen or felt, we know to come to us from the outside through the channels of sense. They make us aware of a "sensation" when we give our attention to them. In like manner there are certain inner disturbances that are recognized by us also as "sensations" — when we give them our attention — and these we are aware, reproduce the original effects of the outside stimuli.

(e). But there are all sorts of vibrations inside and out of our bodies that we fail to recognize as our own personal or inherited experiences because they are either refused our personal attention or they make such slight impressions on our general consciousness that they remain in subconsciousness and never reach us actively.

Yet all these have the same effect on consciousness and leave indelible records and may, under certain circumstances be "re-collected" to serve a purpose. That is it is possible for us to "recollect" "memories" we never knew definitely we had!

(f). This is because, as heretofore pointed out, only a small percentage of our consciousness is Self-defined — that is, only a small percentage of it is Self-consciousness. The rest is not sufficiently coordinated by nerves, and possibly other connections, to become Self-consciousness, without some extra effort on the part of the individual (Self) themselves. It is that non-self-defined consciousness we call "the subconscious" — (subliminal, psychic, subjective and so on).

(g). Normally, humans receive practically all impressions first on sub-consciousness. Thence they flow naturally to one's personal attention if they are powerful enough to do so by themselves. Some that are not so powerful may be detected by concentration of Attention as described in Lesson 1. Others, of too weak a nature to reach further than the first small nerve center or "brain," of the system it affects, lie outside the view of personal attention, like the undiscovered stars evade the most powerful telescope or the atom evades the electron-microscope.

Now, if you will turn back to Lesson 3 on Energy, you will understand that these impressions on human consciousness all produce certain physical effects in the atomic and molecular structure of the cells (especially the nerve cells) of the body generally, that science calls chemical change and chemical reaction. These physical effects result from sudden pulses of 'energy (universal and human) that either release or concentrate energy contained in the cells or their mechanism.

The result of these pulses, waves, pushes and pulls of energy, are to establish **PERMANENT TENDENCIES** all along the route of their action within the body, **TO REPRODUCE THEMSELVES UNDER THE SAME CIRCUMSTANCES WHICH BROUGHT THEM ABOUT.**

A crude analogy is the folding of a perfectly blank sheet of paper. The paper represents consciousness. The fold is a "memory." Once folded, the paper can be straightened out to look like it was before, but it will always fold more easily along the crease made in it than at any other place.

EXPERIMENT IN REMEMBERING

I place an important business document in a "safe place" — and "forget" where I placed it.

Afterward, some apparently unrelated circumstance gives a jog to memory, and I find it. The memory comes suddenly and without warning after I had struggled long and earnestly to "recall it."

I pick up a bundle of old papers and find the document in the last place I would have expected to find it, because "something told" me to look there. The "something" seemed to impart its advice to me while looking over the morning newspaper. Why?

EXPLANATION — When I hid the document, not only was my imagination involved in seeking a safe place where someone else would never expect to find it, but also my sight, hearing and sense of touch. These impressions altogether made up my mental picture of myself hiding that document.

When I read the morning paper, I saw that it was a paper; it had the smell of the bundle of old papers in which I secreted my treasure — and it had the feel. Hence, sub-consciousness was set in motion by these stimuli which were similar to those of my first experience in hiding the document. Although my personal attention was not focused on visualizing all these things while I hid the document, yet the memory record was made and was afterward revived when I read the morning paper — strongly enough to be called a "hunch" (intuition) even though too weak to make me aware of it as **KNOWLEDGE**. I had to sit down and reason the whole thing out by concentrating my attention on the mystery before I gained **KNOWLEDGE** of it.

ASSOCIATION OF IDEAS

This experiment also serves to call attention to the fact that Memory is increased in power and clarity by self-consciously associating one idea with another, so that in "remembering" one of them we will "remember" the other. Here it is that Imagination plays such an important part, in charting and marking the paths taken by impressions on consciousness.

Each sensory impression is represented on this chart as a **TENDENCY** of the mechanism of nerve cells to polarize in a certain way differing slightly from the polarization tendencies set up by every other impression.

We may graphically depict this by drawing a line on a sheet of paper to represent each impression. The line is the symbol of an **IDEA**.

The **IDEA** (mental picture) is an actual or imaginary experience recorded on consciousness. It comes within the definition of **KNOWLEDGE** so far as it resulted from an actual experience and can be analyzed into its original parts when it is the result of imaginary combination of primary ideas.

Therefore, the **IDEA** is as real a **THING** as a photograph or other record. It is material from which we build Thoughts, as we build houses from brick, stone or wood.

Like material massed for building a physical structure, the countless **IDEAS** stored in our consciousness are more or less in contact with each other, because their "lines" cross.

Consider the manner in which an architect goes about building a house and we see at once how the mental architect proceeds to build up a Thought structure — develop an idea — evolve a plan.

The house builder must classify their material and use each class in its proper place. When the house is complete according to the plan of the supervising architect perhaps a dozen or more groups of skilled workmen have been engaged in the work.

So with the mental architect.

YOU ARE THE MASTER BUILDER OF YOUR OWN THOUGHT STRUCTURE.

Your building material is furnished you by Nature. Your consciousness is stored with physical, mental and psychical memories. Imagination enables you to classify them and use them as you **WILL**.

You have the power to connect any idea or set of ideas with any others you desire and use these arbitrary associations in building your business plans — that is, "carry out your ideas in business."

BUT THERE IS NO NECESSITY FOR CREATING IMAGINARY CLASSIFICATIONS OF YOUR IDEAS IN ORDER TO USE THEM PRACTICALLY.

This is very important for the business thinker to know, because teachers of Applied Psychology often go to extremes in devising artificial "Memory Methods." Some of these methods assist and others hinder the methods of Nature.

All of them are limited in efficiency. Most of them are valuable for special purposes only. They all rest on the basis of association of ideas but frequently are such abortions in mental building as to obscure the foundation and prevent its being used for natural memory methods.

There is positive danger in "assisting Nature" by interfering with the natural method of association carried on in subconsciousness, when we proceed on the extravagant claims of some teachers, that artificial classification and association of ideas are the most practical.

The danger lies in developing too great ability to "remember" things at the expense of skill in applying the knowledge practically. It is easy to clutter up the mind with strings of memories that are best left to sub-consciousness. Often these "strings" are not particularly useful.

ATTENTION is kept at work "remembering how to remember" until it has little time to aid Initiative. (See next lesson.)

AVOID ARTIFICIAL MEMORY SYSTEMS

ATTITUDE becomes so largely influenced by the artificial memory systems that its usefulness for most practical purposes becomes impaired. One's latent powers become more and more absorbed in the artificial process of "remembering." We become speculative, more than operative — which is bad for success in business.

If a person wishes merely to qualify as a prodigy of memory or an expert in the art of memorizing long lists of articles, such as a pack of cards, a column of figures or a great number of points they desire to make in a speech, they will find some of the "mental indexes" recommended by modern teachers just the thing. If they expect to make a living by publicly exhibiting themselves and their acquired powers of memory, they can do so with as much justification as the person who earns their living by teaching physical culture methods or who devotes their life to any other profession.

But the average individual in business will find these experts wholly unqualified as a rule, for any other trade or profession. Their prodigious feats of memory do not enable them to manage a business; do not make them executive or financial geniuses. Most of them require "business managers" to succeed in making a living.

The value of the Memory Expert and their place in the business world is simply that of a specialist, an artist, a teacher. And the value of their "system" is merely that of a special time saver for special purposes, just as a card index system is a special time saver for special purposes.

A practical and successful business person will find that they have more time and become more efficient in their business, if they rely more upon the physical system and filing methods devised by office supply houses to suit their particular business, whereby an unlimited number of records and accompanying indexes collected into databases may be used with a key to the whole. If they spend time and energy to reduce all the details of their business to Memory, they will incapacitate themselves for other things.

It is easier and more business like to jot down on a pad of paper (or record in an agenda) the things you want to remember, such as engagements, orders, expenditures, than to commit them to memory. One can do both.

The notes may be filed and referred to with certainty from day to day. One business person employing hundreds of persons once said:

"I NEVER TRUST MY MEMORY, FOR I MIGHT LOSE MY MIND — BUT THE WRITTEN NOTES I MAKE AND FILE ARE READY FOR MY SUCCESSOR IF I DO."

NATURAL ASSOCIATION OF IDEAS

These remarks are not intended to discredit either teachers of special memory systems or their methods, but are intended merely to call attention to the practical limitations of those methods.

IMAGINARY CLASSIFICATION OF IDEAS IS NOT NECESSARY TO MAKE PRACTICAL USE OF THEM.

Ideas are stored in Sub-consciousness when not in Self-conscious use. An Idea once established is classified in Sub-consciousness with an association of similar ideas by the same natural processes that enable the blood stream to convey proper food to each organ and cell group and refuse to deposit any but the proper food at each place.

Sub-consciousness is the most perfect filing system for Ideas, that are possible for humans to conceive. It works automatically with relation to Self-consciousness. Sub-consciousness is intelligent, but lacks the high reasoning power of Self-consciousness. It simply attends to the business of recording, classifying and indexing whatever impressions come into it, as a good librarian would keep a library in order that they might produce at an instant's notice, whatever book is called for.

Your sub-conscious librarian normally works according to a system evolved by Nature, wherein there is a special location for every memory — a special "path" of electrons, atoms, cells, as it were, through which each impression has reached a perceptive center by establishing a tendency of everything in the direct line of that path to "polarize" itself again under the same circumstances that originally made the path.

IT DEPENDS UPON THE AMOUNT OF ATTENTION GIVEN TO THE ORIGINAL CIRCUMSTANCES OR EVENTS FORMING THE IDEA, AS TO HOW STRONG THIS TENDENCY TOWARD RE-POLARIZATION WILL BE. THAT IS, HOW STRONG THE MENTAL PICTURE OF THE IDEA WILL BE, AND CONSEQUENTLY THE GREATER THE DEGREE OF ATTENTION THE EASIER WILL BE THE SUBSEQUENT PROCESS OF RECALLING THE MEMORY (STORED UP IDEA).

"MEMORY" WORKS WHILE YOU SLEEP

If you doubt this, select some business problem whose solution seems to evade you during your waking hours — and go to sleep thinking about it. Make the resolution you will work on it while asleep.

In the morning you will be surprised to find that what seemed a jumble of ideas before, now appears systematically arranged.

You can briefly "command yourself" (really you command "Sub-consciousness") to solve the problem and then "forget it" until some time has elapsed, (hours or days as the case may be), when the solution seems to "pop into your mind."

Sleeping or waking, your sub-conscious activities never cease, for if they did your heart would cease beating and all your physical apparatus cease functioning together. So, when you refer a problem to sub-consciousness and "forget it" as a self-conscious thing, you are simply turning over to it a chaos of its own records to get straightened out. There is no more mystery about it than there is as to the ability of a watchmaker to repair a watch you have ignorantly misused.

When the period of sleep seems to render you "unconscious," because you have no personal (self-conscious) recollection of what transpired during sleep, Sub-consciousness, like a faithful clerk, is busy at work with its natural methods of untangling what **YOU** have tangled. Moreover, its task is performed without the handicap of your personal interference! In sound, healthy sleep, your personal attention is either dormant or otherwise occupied.

HOW YOU CONFUSE YOURSELF

During your waking, working hours, you sometimes confuse sub-consciousness by the many vacillations of reason. Every choice you make of a course of action, is a command to sub-consciousness to fix its attitude accordingly. Every "change of mind" on your part is a command to subconsciousness to change its attitude. Subconsciousness is pulled here and there like the automaton it is, by the directing power of your Will. It has no power to resist you if it wanted to — which it does not because it has no will of its own. Its prime duty is to obey you.

All day, during business hours, Subconsciousness is in a turmoil trying to follow your lead, as you struggle with reason and your concentrated powers of attention, to fit the pieces of a puzzle in your business affairs together, you are impressing Sub-consciousness with one outstanding and overwhelming desire — to solve your problem — to make the pieces fit —

TO FIND THEIR NATURAL RELATION.

This desire on your part, however, is accompanied by no opportunity for subconsciousness to assert itself — to work without the handicap of your constant interference, in performing the work for which it is by Nature specially fitted — namely, of finding that natural relation by the simple process of putting all ideas back into their original relations and then establishing the additional relations between them you were hunting for.

But when you "sleep over the problem," you give Sub-consciousness its opportunity to work in Silence and without handicaps. And it does the work perfectly. Which further illustrates the value of Lesson 4 on Silence.

HOW TO BECOME "CARE FREE"

The business person who will make a habit of leaving their "worries" to the subconscious in this way, will soon develop an amazing ability to "throw aside care" after business hours, that will gradually result in ability to solve the most intricate business difficulties during sleep.

When they have gotten this far, they will be convinced that subconscious thought is a power of tremendous utility. But by continuing the habit they will find even more astonishing revelations in store — from ones own mind.

As sub-consciousness is given more and more freedom of action, it develops great facility and speed in arriving at solutions. There comes a time when its task is finished so quickly the solution is brought to one's personal attention during sleep. The sleeper is at rest physically and yet knows they are awake! As a rule, when this occurs, the sleeper wakes up physically, though if they choose to can continue to "sleep" and at the same time examine the solution brought to them by the subconscious.

The great difference between Nature's methods of associating ideas and those of teachers of applied psychology is that while the latter may prove faulty, the former never does. It is infallible when allowed perfect freedom of action. It cannot produce miracles or "supernatural" effects, but it does its work perfectly with the material furnished it.

AS TO SPECIAL MEMORY SYSTEMS

One of the nearest approaches to the natural methods of subconsciousness yet devised by humanity as an "aid" to Memory is as follows:

A list of incongruous objects is committed to memory, and each connected to the next one by some absurd association of ideas (the more absurd the better) in an imaginary picture string in this way:

1. Hat

2. Hen

3. Ham

4. Wire

5. Hall

6. Shoe

7. Key

8. Bee

9. Hive.

This serves as a "mental index." The hat is the first card because the letter **T** is a single downward stroke. We imagine it to be an enormous animated hat trying to catch the Hen, which is the second card because its last letter **N** represents 2 (two dozen strokes). The hen is the size of an ostrich and pecking at a frantically excited ham — (**M** has three down strokes). And so Wire is 4 because its last letter is the last letter of **FOUR**; **L** represents 5 obviously because in Roman numerals **L** is 50 and the **"O"** is not counted — being nothing! Shoe has the **S** sound of six and its last letter is the figure 6 turned topsy-turvy; Key is 7 because 7 is a mystical number; Bee has the form of 8; Hive is closely associated with Bee and is, therefore, 9. And so any number of words may be symbolized, visualized, animated and worked into the string of pictures.

(You will note in passing that the only naturally connected words in the list are Hive and Bee!)

After remembering this index which is to help us remember other things we may connect with it, we are prepared to remember how to remember. For instance a pack of 52 cards can be remembered by associating each of the pack with one of the first 52 items of our index. Long columns of figures can be in like manner remembered and added or subtracted. Mental indexes can be contrived to enable one to achieve the most remarkable mental feats of memory.

A good example of a person capable of exceptional feats of memory was a person, who was said to be so slow in his youth that it took him nine years to complete the fourth grade in school BUT later he became regarded as the champion memory expert of America, through use of this kind of system. His name was Charles W. Hamley, and he went on to become a well respected teacher at the University of Southern California, so one account says.

During the first world war, he carried coded messages, inventoried great invoices of railway supplies and did other feats for the American Army in France — all without taking down written notes. It is said to have taken a corps of army clerks a week to transcribe one list of supplies he committed to memory.

Hamley's most significant conclusion as to his own powers was quoted by Jack Jungmeyer, a Los Angeles news writer at the time, as follows:

ADVICE OF A MEMORY EXPERT

"Things you yourself have done are easiest to recall. Things you have seen are next easiest. Things read or acquired second hand are not so intimate or vivid. Hence **THEY MUST BE TRANSLATED INTO PERSONAL EXPERIENCE** by imaginary pictures and mental action."

"I literally have thousands of long picture chains, embracing a wide range of knowledge, securely tied to my mental hitching post, to be released at will."

"If you want to remember an accurate description of a building mentally climb it like a human spider, grasping each cornice, peering in at the windows, tearing your fingernails on the bricks. If you feel the exploit and thrill to it, you'll remember that building in detail always."

"If the name of a person isn't impressive to you, substitute a familiar and simpler name. **CONCENTRATE** for ten or twenty seconds on the difference and similarity. Mentally file Mr. Tuttle as Mr. Turtle, which links him to a familiar image."

"Try acting out a poem with appropriate and exaggerated gestures and see how it helps fix and fit the words together."

These conclusions when attentively studied should suggest to you a fact that most memory experts seem to overlook — that nature's methods must be the base of all true memory systems.

A T T E N T I O N ("concentration") TO THE ACTION, TIME AND PLACE OF AN EVENT, IS THE BEST WAY TO FIX IT IN YOUR MEMORY. YOUR OWN PERSONAL ACTION, MENTAL OR PHYSICAL, IS THE MOST EASILY REMEMBERED. THEREFORE REDUCE EVERYTHING YOU SEE, HEAR OR OF MENTAL ACTION. IF YOU OTHERWISE SENSE, TO TERMS, GIVE THIS ACTION DUE ATTENTION YOU WILL NOT NEED TO CLASSIFY BY

AN ARTIFICIAL CODE. THE REGULAR SEQUENCE OF YOUR OWN PERSONAL EXPERIENCES FROM DAY TO DAY IS NATURE'S CODE — AND NATURE NEVER FORGETS.

AN EXPERIMENT

To illustrate the manner in which Nature's method may be used constantly by a busy person, try the following:

When you get up tomorrow morning start giving your attention to the day's activities. Let nothing you wish to remember escape your attention. Do not slow up in your work or play, but see that you do it all intensely and put your whole energy and attention into it.

At the end of the day, sit or lie in a relaxed condition of mind and body and retrace your day's work and play step by step. You will be surprised to discover how much you remember. It unfolds in your imagination before your "mind's eye" like a panorama or a movie.

Attention is the whole secret. Subconsciousness attends to the recording. The next day's activities will be linked to those of this day without a break. Sleep is no break in the chain. Sound sleep merely diverts attention that is divided between sub-consciousness and self-consciousness during waking and physically active hours, wholly to the use of subconsciousness.

PRACTICE THE FOLLOWING EXERCISE DAILY

Memory — At the end of the day, exercise your memory by retracing your actions and observations of the morning as outlined under the subject of Attention, above. Since Memory measures the degree of Attention you exercised in the morning you will find the checking-up process of the afternoon or night, will help you cultivate attention. As you cultivate this habit, you will eventually so cultivate your memory that you will be able instantly to recall anything you did, said or heard or observed during the day. You will become more efficient in your work, for you will not lose time because of forgetting things.

Recall daily to memory, everything done or observed by you during some fixed period of time during the day, however short.

You may vary the exercise of course.

Therefore, commit to memory at least one name of a business acquaintance per day. Mentally visualize their appearance, the most outstanding thing you have seen them do. Connect these ideas with their name — say their name is **COOK**. You see them mentally as they are

"COOKING" up some business affair that has attracted your attention, or as a **COOK** in their office or in some other place stamped on your memory that you know they have been — they are dressed as a **COOK** in a rather extravagant costume.

For example perhaps, the next day, you treat your friend or acquaintance **PHILLIPS** the same way. He is a banker, flipping the coins he counts in his bank. See the play on words.

10

LESSON VIII

INITIATIVE

Greater business rewards come to those people who are "self-actors" — who "start things" — than to those whose activities have to be directed by others. Such "self-starters" we call people of Initiative.

It has been the purpose of the foregoing seven lessons to point out to the student the nature of their mental equipment so that they may use it intelligently in starting themselves off on the road to success.

Mere thinking, however "right" the thought is, will get you nowhere without starting, any more than a driver in an automobile will get to the next town just by sitting in it and wishing the car would move of its own accord. You have the knowledge of HOW to start your car.

INITIATIVE IS THE APPLICATION OF KNOWLEDGE

You have just learned,

I. That Attention is the first essential to success in business.

II. That through Attention you may establish a correct mental Attitude toward your work and fellow-workers.

III. That Energy follows Attention, and the direction of its flow is determined by Attitude which, in turn, is determined by Attention.

IV. That Silence is the conserver of Energy because it aids in concentrating Attention and prevents disturbance of Attitude.

V. That Vision is best cultivated in Silence and is the first step toward Initiative.

VI. That Emotion arouses Vision which is then shaped into practical design through Imagination, presenting you with a variety of plans and methods for accomplishing your desires, one of which you select by the power of Will (the choosing faculty as the executive authority of the mind), which you give proper Attention until your purpose is accomplished. (See next lesson on Purpose.) That Emotion is **POWER**.

VII. That Memory is the storehouse of material for Vision and is evidence of the degree of Attention. That it is the one thing that makes Emotion possible. That it is the clerical department of your general Consciousness. That if you cultivate (use) Memory you become more responsive to Emotion and by controlling Emotion you develop Vision. If you have Vision, you can act upon your own Initiative with intelligence.

INITIATIVE A DIRECTING POWER

The business world always welcomes with open arms the individual who has Initiative — who acts without being told — who doesn't have to be "bossed" — who can tell others what to do and how to do it when they do not know.

Such people inevitably rise to positions of trust and responsibility. They become the executives of the world.

Those without Initiative, just as inevitably remain in subordinate positions and are easily influenced to envy of those with Initiative, because, in their ignorance of natural law, they do not comprehend that **INTELLIGENCE ALWAYS GOVERNS IGNORANCE.** Nature has provided that it be so. Otherwise, humanity would be wholly subject to physical force, and the "survival of the fittest" would mean the survival of the physically strongest.

History and observation demonstrate that the "fittest" humans survive, because they are the most intelligent — which may not be a great degree of intelligence compared with the intelligence of the highest thinkers it is true; yet even today we find that those races who are most intelligent in their use of physical force, invariably win over those who are less intelligent in such use.

HOW TO APPLY INITIATIVE

Whatever your trade, business or profession and whatever your present position in it may be, if you have thoroughly mastered the principles set forth in these lessons and applied them to yourself, you have now developed potential powers of Initiative that will take you up in the business world as rapidly as you release this power to perform work.

That is the Natural Law.

For example: suppose you are a common laborer and have never been used to anything in your life except to work as you were directed, in a gang of laborers like yourself, unskilled, unambitious, unthinking — content to do the day's task, draw the day's wage and spend whatever surplus there may be after paying for food and shelter, on such pleasures as you are capable of enjoying.

Then you develop Initiative.

Your Initiative can no more be concealed than the fact that you have hands and feet. It has become part of **YOU**. Others will see it as part of your "Character." They will observe that you have more than average intelligence.

You will be impelled, by the very fact that you have powers of Initiative to use those powers when emergency arises — just as you instinctively protect yourself from a blow or rush to save a fellow human from threatened death.

When there is necessity for someone to take charge of a group of your fellow workers to assist the foreman, you are picked for the job, probably at their insistence. This may or may not be "friendship" on their part, for they are impelled by their own account to associate with them the most efficient people. Your Initiative is your advertisement to the foreman of your efficiency.

If you happen to be the best available "section boss" when a foreman is needed — you get the place. You get higher positions when you go after them and demonstrate you are the best person for the job — all because you exercise your powers of Initiative.

Granted that a worker has the right Attitude, concentrates Attention on the job before them and has Initiative, their advancement in business becomes almost a matter of geometrical progression.

Do not attempt to deceive yourself, however, that you have Initiative, if you are conscious that any element of success is lacking in you. Initiative demands the most unremitting Attention to the business at hand. If you have not the element of Attention implanted in your being, you have not true Initiative.

You will only be regarded as a "false alarm" by others. The so-called "genius" that starts something and then quits because they cannot concentrate their attention on the job, is not the sort of person with Initiative the business world is looking for. They merely show a flash of Initiative.

Initiative that wins success, demands that you not only be eternally ready and fit, but that you watch your opportunities and "take the Initiative" in seizing them. An old saw says that "all things come to the one who waits," but unless you have Initiative you are not likely to see opportunity when it does come — much less grasp it.

Initiative, the power to apply knowledge, gets you nowhere by waiting. You must Act.

ACTION IS THE ESSENCE OF INITIATIVE

Applying the principle of Initiative to the lessons, you have already learned you will observe the following facts.

1. You are chiefly interested in finding Opportunity for advancement. Initiative impels you to connect with Opportunity, and if there is none in sight, to **MAKE ONE**.

2. When Opportunity is found or made, Initiative demands that you focus Attention upon it; that your Attitude be one of receptiveness toward it — a readiness to take full advantage of the Opportunity.

3. Initiative will demand the most efficient and economical use of all your Energies to work out all the possibilities of Opportunity. Silence conserves energy, so that Initiative must never be boastful but must work out its plans, ideas and theories in Silence.

4. Initiative demands constantly increased Vision and continually greater control of Emotion. Hence, it is obvious that Emotion, which is power, must not only be controlled, but fed as you would feed your body. Memory and experience are the foods of Emotion. The person of Initiative, therefore, is one who intensifies and speeds up their whole life. They attentively observe everything that goes on around them. They never miss an opportunity to investigate anything connected with their business or which their active Imagination can picture as possible in such connection.

5. These applications of Initiative create Opportunity — or to be more exact, make Opportunity more apparent.

Throughout every department of the business world, the person of Initiative is known as a "Live Wire."

VALUE OF A SOCIAL LIFE

That is why successful business people spend time and money in club life, where they daily learn something of the psychology of their fellows. That is why they seem to "be in everything" — to make as many social, fraternal, banking and other connections as they can.

They regard these connections as worth while and the money spent in maintaining them as capital wisely invested, because it brings them in daily contact with some new experience, and experience is knowledge that may be usefully applied through Initiative in the future.

The person of Initiative gradually comes to see the business world in perspective, as it were. They see it as a **UNITY** in which they have a definite and important place and a necessary task to perform.

They discover for themselves that "Business" is but the exchange of one kind of service for another kind of service. Their viewpoint of things becomes greater, and they become greater.

They find that "Business" is the natural consequence of human evolution and increased civilization; that it is but another form of that ideal of "Universal Humanity" that is a fact in Nature which people so badly imitate in their dealings with each other.

The "Live Wires" of business very soon discover their own importance to the conduct of the family affairs of humanity — and if they sometimes grow a bit conceited, they injure no one but themselves. They succeed by doing a large amount of extra work — mental, physical, or both — when they find that the great majority of their brother workers seem entirely willing for the "live wires" to shoulder their burdens and assume their responsibilities — though these same brother workers, as a rule, complain loudly that the Live Wires also reap the benefits.

It is the person of Initiative who becomes the authority on organization, in commerce, finance, sociology, government, and on how to use the uncontrolled forces of Nature, including human energy, for human comfort and their own profit.

Initiative often applies the knowledge of other people without Initiative — to the intense disgust of those whose knowledge is used because it is idle. That is Nature's way of rebuking all who are too lazy to use her gifts.

Idle knowledge should no more be wasted than physical machinery. Knowledge belongs to humanity. If its individual possessor will not use it for the good of humanity, then they cannot complain if others do so.

The person of Initiative wastes nothing themselves, and when they find others throwing away what they can use — they just appropriate it sometimes without much thought on the ethics of their actions.

Some dreamer invents a thing that will benefit all humanity. They make no effort to produce, advertise, or market it. The "live wire" gathers it up and makes millions of dollars out of it for themselves by finishing the work the dreamer left undone.

Then the inventor and their friends complain of the injustice, bad faith and bad ethics of the "live wire." Their complaint is often well founded for persons of Initiative, while possessing all the other elements of success, often lack just one — the right Attitude.

Such a person rarely looks into the future because their Vision is impaired, so they do not realize until the thing happens, that they will have to pay for the injustice done the inventor in the theft of their invention. If they did realize it, they would perhaps "take a chance" just the same, regarding a "bird in the hand as worth two in the bush."

The person of Initiative may care nothing for ethics — and they can be truly successful in life only so far as they; do indeed, pay attention to the ethics of business; they may adopt a wrong Attitude in their relations with the rest of the human family — and inevitably pay for it in loss of happiness; they may be lacking in many ways for a completely successful business life.

But they are, nevertheless, the most essential factor in human progress so far as the business of carrying on the upward struggle of the race toward civilization is concerned. No student of success in business can afford to overlook Initiative or leave it out of their calculations.

It is Initiative that has furnished us with all our explorers, pioneers, inventors and others who have "done things" good or bad, in the world.

PRACTICE THE FOLLOWING EXERCISE DAILY

Initiative — Each day, select some difficulty in your work, if there are any, and in **SILENCE** try to **VISION** a way out. Then **TRY** out the solution your imagination presents you. Try always to do something thoroughly and well. Make it something that no one else has done or been doing. Take the initiative, even if it is nothing more than cleaning up your own place of work — left for the office boy who has not done it.

11

LESSON IX

PURPOSE

Have **PURPOSE** in all you do, if you would attain success.

Purpose is the North Pole of Attitude.

Anyone who so chooses, can climb from out of poverty to independence if that is their fixed purpose.

Poverty and independence are like two villages many miles apart. To get from one to the other is simply a matter of locomotion and direction.

Four things are necessary to locomotion.

First, the determination to go.

Second, a means of transportation.

Third, the action of "going."

Fourth, the direction you go.

I determine to go from Pittsburgh to New York.

Having no automobile and no money, I use my legs and walk. If I am crippled, the journey may be a bit painful and take longer than riding, but I will get to New York if I have to drag myself on hands and knees, because that was my purpose from the start. If I am blind or deaf or dumb, I run extra dangers by the way — but I will get to New York if I live.

So, the journey from Poverty to Financial Independence may be begun and finished by any individual whose Purpose remains steadfast, even if they are crippled for lack of initial knowledge or is deaf and dumb or blind to some of the natural principles of success set forth in these lessons.

Obviously, the journey must be a long and toilsome one to those who, for example, are blinded by prejudice, ignorance, superstition, dogma and "stand-pat-ism" of the character that refuses to recede from a position once assumed. These things affect one's attitude. You may get started in the wrong direction, away from your Purpose. You may go forward blindly from Poverty into Anarchy before you get your bearings.

BUT IT YOU HAVE PURPOSE YOU WILL ACHIEVE IT BY CONTINUAL TRIAL.

Your Purpose, of course, may be evil and destructive, in which event you will not be successful in Business in the way most business people understand the term. But you will undoubtedly be successful in accomplishing the evil and destruction you have set your mind to, at least so far as relates to its consequences on **YOU**. In other words you are at liberty to commit business suicide if you wish.

However, we will here consider that the **PURPOSE** you have in mind is business success; that the success you wish is in your own particular business; that you are not now crippled or maimed mentally because you have applied to your affairs the lessons of Attention, Attitude, Energy, Silence, Vision, Emotion, Memory, and Initiative; or if you still are deficient in application of some of these principles, that you possess intelligence enough to correct these deficiencies yourself.

You have the means of transportation, therefore, to any point in the business world you wish. But you must **USE** those means. And it is up to you, whether you ride or walk. All you have to do to ride, is to generate your own power, pull the lever after aiming your machine toward your Purpose and pay strict attention to the rules of the road — the lessons you have just been reviewing.

As you apply them to your own situation, you will find that you have to use just so much power to cover so much ground.

Laying aside figurative language, you find you must earn your way in the business world. You must pay for everything you get — even credit has to be paid for. No one ever gets something for nothing, however inadequate the price they seem to pay at the time.

The standard of value in the business world is a single and universal standard — and the dollar is not that standard.

SERVICE IS THE UNIT OF VALUE IN BUSINESS.

THE DOLLAR IS MERELY ONE OF ITS SYMBOLS — A MEDIUM OF EXCHANGE. SERVICE, THEREFORE, MUST BE THE ULTIMATE PURPOSE OF THOSE WHO WOULD SUCCEED IN BUSINESS.

We exchange a service for a service.

A yard of goods represents so much service to humanity by the maker of it. Every article of merchandise represents a part of the general service of all individuals to collective humanity. All work performed and things produced are parts of this Service.

A pair of shoes, a pound of sugar, a bag of groceries, or a day's work, all are part of the sum total of service that humanity owes itself — that Nature demands as the price of life and civilization.

Looking with clear eyes at the facts, we find that we owe life, just what we get out of it. This view is important to the business person, for it is a sad fact that the majority of people appear to think that life owes them a living; that society is under some sort of obligation to the individual to keep them alive, no matter how lazy they are.

Whereas, society really owes no one a living unless they earn it. Nature owes them nothing they refuse to pay for.

If we fail in our individual duty as workers, we know that someone else must shoulder our burdens and responsibilities. The individual who does not serve in some way, is like a dead cell in the body of humanity.

This sounds like religion or philosophy — it is business religion and business philosophy. It is Truth. It has been demonstrated time and again. Without the **PURPOSE** of Service, there can be no progress.

To receive, we must give. To get out of Life, we must put into Life.

When I pay money for clothes, food, shelter, amusement or anything else that has taken the service of one or more of my fellows to produce, I am but exchanging the symbol of an equivalent service. I have earned that money by Service, or by selling some product of Service. Else I am using money that represents stored up Service performed by another.

Because our civilization becomes more complicated as we advance in it, we lose sight of this primary fact of Service for Service, under a mass of detail and symbol. We become specialists in Service — merchants, lawyers, carpenters, day laborers. Attention is divided between our own part of the world's work and other things. We adopt an Attitude toward our own work and toward other things and workers, that magnifies our part and minimizes theirs. And so, we forget that to **RECEIVE** we must

GIVE.

WE HAVE BECOME CONFUSED OVER THE QUESTION OF MONEY

We have even garbled the words of one of the greatest teachers of Business ethics that ever lived — a teacher of a race that has taught the western world all it now knows of Business.

Our moralists have said, "Money Is the Root of All Evil."

The teacher said, "The Love of Money Is the Root of All Evil."

We have garbled the ancient advice of the teacher in order to explain to ourselves why some people accumulate great piles of money they could not possibly earn through their own service — fabulous amounts that grow and grow far beyond the ability of the possessor and their entire family to spend in a lifetime on earth. We talk about the unequal distribution of wealth as though Money constituted wealth. We want to explain how it is possible for one individual to have so much and another to have so little, when both, perhaps, do the same amount of work — perform the same amount of service.

All this results from the distraction of Attention to individual Service, with a consequent confusion of Attitude toward Service — which means that we fail of Purpose, either because our distracted Attention does not see Purpose clearly, or our confused Attitude is turned from any definite Purpose.

In the nature of things, there must be **ONE ROAD** to success that is shortest and common sense tells us to take that one. To take this one road we must use all our latent powers, faculties and capacities one hundred percent. How to do this, these lessons tell. But they cannot tell you more. They cannot clear away the obstacles you will find in your path — of which, perhaps, the greatest is the wrong Attitude different individuals take toward "Money."

Since Attitude governs the direction, we will take toward Purpose, and business people with different Attitudes will naturally take different directions — some away from and some directly toward success. Some will take circuitous routes to arrive at the goal, learning through their mistakes. Others will head straight for it — to miss the goal at last through some trivial bypath that lures them from their course.

Therefore, we see honorable and intelligent people end their lives in poverty, and we see great scoundrels amass great wealth, because the honorable person utterly fails to devote their Attention to the simple fundamentals of success and the scoundrel takes advantage of their ignorance by appropriating that which the honorable person leaves unguarded.

The Selfish or Greedy individual would never be able to dominate the unselfish and liberal one, if due Attention were given to the laws of success by those who render the best Service. The unequal division of wealth in the world is primarily due to the carelessness of those who suffer from it most.

The dreamer, the altruist, the individual who devotes their life to Service, cares little for the material rewards that are rightfully theirs. This does not do away with the fact that this person IS entitled to these rewards. So, when, as usually happens, old age creeps up on them, with those dependent upon them unprovided for this person is inclined to rail at the "injustice" of it all, without the least suspicion that only this person has themselves to blame for being at fault.

This person has bartered not only their own just returns for work done, but those of their loved ones, for the personal pleasure of giving — a beautiful and sentimental viewpoint, like that of Goldsmith's Vicar of Wakefield, but a most uncomfortable and unjust situation for the victims of their — **EMOTIONALISM**.

MONEY is no evil. It is the symbol of Service performed by someone.

If you wish to describe the Purpose of Business as "the making of Money," do so with the understanding that Business is the mutual exchange of Service.

THE GREAT BUSINESS PURPOSE IS SERVICE

- A dollar earned is a service earned.

- A dollar saved is a service saved.

- Those who earn are workers.

- Those who save are capitalists.

- Labor and Capital are one and the same thing — Service.

- The **PURPOSE** of both is — Service.

- So, we see, that Service is the ultimate purpose of all Business — that it must be, because,

- Service is the product of Energy.

- Energy is directed by Attention.

- Attention determines Attitude.

- Attitude determines business success.

All promotion comes through Service of someone, yourself or another whose Service you appropriate. The cheerful personal service you give is the most efficient Purpose you could have in life for it is the thing that wins promotion, custom, friends.

When an individual begins to Serve cheerfully, they **ARE** a business success.

PRACTICE THE FOLLOWING EXERCISE DAILY

Purpose — EACH DAY SELECT SOMETHING YOU INTEND TO DO, AND THEN DO IT. Never put off doing the thing. Form your purpose in the morning and set a time to perform it. If it is to go fishing, then go fishing. You will thereby cultivate a habit of forming purposes and of achieving them. This is the habit of quick action, of keeping your word.

12

LESSON X

AMBITION

To "get ahead" and to "do something bigger" seems to be the natural ambition of everyone in business. There is always an impelling desire to surpass all previous success, that seems to pull or push the business person from one achievement to another.

When one purpose is accomplished, another and greater purpose immediately crystallizes for the ambitious people.

This is because **AMBITION IS THE ACTIVE CONSEQUENCE OF VISION.**

The mental sequence is as follows:

(a). Pleasurable emotion follows any successful achievement, because success satisfies something that was lacking to our happiness.

(b). This emotion (which remember, is power) brings out from memory, pictures of past achievements (or attempts to achieve) for comparison, by attention, with the present achievement.

(c). Attention finds, by comparison, that one achievement is naturally, greater than another; usually the last achievement being the greatest — that is, having given the greatest personal satisfaction. But it also, naturally and inevitably, discovers that the achievement, however successful and satisfactory, is not yet the **ULTIMATE** measure of personal satisfaction.

(d). This discovery is made, because Imagination, which is engaged in forming the picture images under scrutiny of Attention, insists on building an ideal picture of what could or might be achieved and presenting that composite production for comparison also, with what has actually been achieved.

(e). Hence, the emotion (desire) is aroused within us, of wanting that ideal, because possibly, it seems to be the one thing we lack. We have the feeling that something is yet lacking to complete satisfaction — we **KNOW** that our success **MIGHT** be greater — that it is **POSSIBLE** for us to achieve more than we have done. This is Vision.

(f). There may be a vision of several possibilities for greater achievement and therefore of several desires. When the **WILL** makes a choice of these, the desire or wish becomes **PURPOSE** and we are drawn to that purpose by Ambition.

We See — and we Want; that is Ambition.

We determine to have what we want — that is Ambition.

AMBITION A YOUTH-PRESERVING FORCE

Ambition is Nature's way of urging us ever forward to help her to complete ourselves by achieving self-satisfaction and success. So long as we have a spark of Ambition, we know that the world still has some use for us and that Nature still thinks it worth while to come to our aid.

When we become entirely satisfied with ourselves and lose all Ambition, we are ready to be cast out as a mentally dried up and useless cell in the body of humanity.

Ambition, being a complex of emotions, is, like all other emotions, a "mover out of the mind." As such, it is a force, a power, that rightly used and kept under control, can be directed like any other force, physical or mental, for the accomplishment of specific results.

Untrained thinkers are often full of uncontrolled "ambitions" that are not entirely clear to them. They only know that they are full of unsatisfied desires — but are not fully aware just what these desires are! This is because the untrained thinker has not learned to focus their attention on their own desires, one after another so that they gain a clear view of them, their causes and their possible effects.

These budding ambitions arise from and have their roots in sub-consciousness. And, as it is from sub-consciousness and its stores of memory we must draw our material for Vision, it is obvious that Ambition and Vision should grow together.

Only unsatisfied desires can provide us with an Ambition. The full-blown Ambition is a complex of various other emotions perhaps — a focus of emotional "rays" as it were — a composite, unsatisfied desire that demands satisfaction of **US**. The desire is so urgent — so overwhelming — so importunate, that we decide to gratify it, because we feel that gratification will give us personal pleasure, satisfaction, content.

And, as in the case of the sub-conscious physical emotions of hunger and thirst, which are also urgent, overwhelming, importunate, it is Self-consciousness that must set about finding means to gratify Ambition.

ANALYZE YOUR AMBITIONS

To do this, we must first precisely discover what it is that we are Ambitious for by applying Attention, examining Attitude, using Energy, working in Silence and constructing Vision that satisfies the conditions demanded by Ambition.

When we turn Attention to an analysis of the minor emotions that go to make up Ambition, we find some very strange things.

Fear of poverty, fear of remaining in our present status where so many desires are unsatisfied, and fear of a good many other things, enter into Ambition. Therefore, it must be some positive thing that will attract this negative emotion forward — or some negative thing behind it that repulses it and sends it forward.

Love of those dependent upon us is also an incentive to Ambition. Therefore, this positive emotion must either have some negative thing — some obstacle to be removed for instance — in front of it to attract it forward or it must have some positive thing — such as danger to those loved ones — behind it to repulse it and send it forward.

Fear and Love are exact opposites. Both represent **POWER**; when controlled and directed, this power enables us to achieve our ambitions. Under the natural law that impels everything to seek vibratory correspondence with something else like itself but of opposite polarity, these two potent energies reinforce each other.

So, our complex emotion of Ambition is one of the most powerful forces we have with which to win business success. It literally pushes us away from failure and the past and pulls us forward into the future toward success. Arising from subconsciousness, it must be controlled by Self to be permanently beneficial. Alexander the Great and Napoleon were examples of temporarily successful individuals, who failed at the last because they did not subject Ambition to Self-control.

AMBITION MUST BE CONTROLLED

When we let Ambition control, we may appear to others to be successful, but we are painfully conscious that to ourselves we are rank failures. We gain the hollow shell but not the kernel of success. For it is the knowledge that **WE** and none other, are the victors, that makes achievement so sweet. That which we receive without giving anything in return, never has the satisfying effect that something that has caused us a struggle, or an expenditure of energy, gives.

AMBITION IMPELS US TO BUILD, WHEN WE CONTROL IT.

UNCONTROLLED, AMBITION MAY CAUSE US TO DESTROY WHEN WE OUGHT TO BUILD — TO SURRENDER PRINCIPLE WHEN WE OUGHT TO HOLD IT FAST — TO LOSE THE SUBSTANCE OF SUCCESS IN OUR EAGERNESS FOR THE APPEARANCE.

Ambition, being a condensed group of emotions, may be compared to a storage battery carried around by an intelligent individual through every department of the human mechanism, for the purpose of filling those parts brim full of energy where they are not already full. This is not strange, because emotion is power, energy, force.

It therefore reinforces and speeds up the whole system, mentally and physically. It demands action and furnishes the power for action. It is at once a dynamo, a transformer, a concentrator and a transmitter of energy.

As long as you can keep Attention focused on Ambition, you can feed its emotions; cause them to grow by receiving constant stimulus at the very source of emotions; keep them concentrated and rightly directed.

A VEGETABLE ANALOGY

It is rather difficult, because of the inadequate language we have, to make clear the scientific fact that **AMBITION** is like a growing plant — with roots in a soil that furnishes it food; and stalk and leaves in an atmosphere that enables it to breathe and grow toward the sunlight; that it may be cultivated like a plant and made to produce the fruit of success.

To illustrate:

Fear and Love and other emotions that go to make up the complex of Ambition, have their roots in Poverty and Desire to Serve respectively. These then, are the soils that furnish food for Ambition's growth. Poverty repels and forces ambition upward. Love attracts, therefore, draws

Ambition upward. It is your own personal atmosphere in which Ambition grows toward the sun of Purpose you are determined to be successful in accomplishing.

Were we to cut off the roots, so that we could efface the memory of Poverty for example or erase the desire for Service from our minds, we would thereby kill our plant by depriving it of its food sources.

AMBITION IS A MENTAL PLANT GROWTH AND LIKE THE PLANT IS A TRANSFORMER OF LOWER COARSER ENERGIES INTO HIGHER AND FINER FORCES.

This being so, we may use Imagination to draw a more intimate picture.

Every plant needs a constant supply of food. Emotion is the food supply of our mental plant — Ambition.

RENEW YOUR EMOTIONAL LIFE FREQUENTLY

Hence, to keep Ambition in a healthy condition the Emotions which are the soil for its roots, need constant stimulation and control. This means that **WE MUST NEVER "FORGET" THE THINGS THAT "AROUSED AMBITION" IF WE WOULD KEEP AMBITION ALIVE.**

It is well to renew our emotional life at frequent intervals — not our "emotionalism" which is the result of permitting emotion to control us. This may be done in a variety of ways — by reading books, attending theaters, listening to lectures, music, poetry, viewing great paintings, cultivating the love of art and the beautiful; and above all by little personal journeys back into the world from which your own Ambition is lifting you or has lifted you.

As everything we do, say or think arouses emotion, we can go even further and obtain powerful emotional reactions which we can store away as energy by personal contact with people and things in which we live the stories we like to read, the plays we like to see. A generous personal action produces an emotion more powerful than any that arises from reading or witnessing a play.

To exercise your Emotions in this way is to generate power — to keep constantly green in your memory the reasons for your Ambition; to strengthen that Ambition and that Memory.

The result is literally to bring a fresh flow of vital forces into your mental plant of Ambition and to make it grow.

THE ADVERTISING REPRESENTATIVE ILLUSTRATES

As an illustration, let us suppose you are in the advertising business. Your ambition is to be one of the most original and successful advertising experts in your field. You are "full of ideas" at times, because you have a vivid imagination that constantly makes new combinations of your own mental pictures.

There are times when you feel yourself mentally exhausted, however. Ideas seem difficult of production — that is new and "original" ones. What do you do? Perhaps you take a walk through the city or out into the country "seeking inspiration." You hope to find something, a sight or sound maybe, that will start some new train of thought leading to an original idea? Why?

Because you instinctively recognize the fact that your emotions need stimulating. You attend a convention of advertising representatives or go to your advertising club and come away mentally strong and fresh. You have been "filled up with ideas" because others have "exchanged ideas" with you. Some great speaker perhaps, "arouses your Imagination"— which is to say, renews your emotional activity.

Every business person, for this reason, must "keep up with the times" and with what is going on in their profession, if they expect to be successful in their Ambition to go higher.

WHY AMBITION ACCEPTS NO OBSTACLES

When you grasp these ideas, you will find that you can use Ambition as you would use an electric torch or some other powerful flame for burning and melting your way through obstacles and for welding together things necessary to success that are otherwise difficult to join.

A person with Ambition is a person with something more than even a Self-confidence that believes they can succeed. This person **KNOWS** they will succeed! They recognize that **THEY** are absolute master of their own fate and that nothing but themselves is able to stop their progress so long as they live.

This is not egotism. It is but the knowledge they have acquired by Attention to the development of their own latent powers.

To tell such an individual that they cannot do a thing causes that same person the same kind of amusement a parent would have if their child told them that they could not step over a two-foot hedge that, a hedge that seemed to the child to be too high.

Ambition pays small attention to critics. So feed your Ambition — but control it. The master key of success is **SELF-CONTROL**.

PRACTICE THE FOLLOWING EXERCISE DAILY

Ambition — ASK YOURSELF EACH DAY WHAT YOU WOULD MOST LIKE TO ACHIEVE. Stimulate your Ambition in this way. Crystallize it into purpose. Then work to achieve it.

Select some business person, whom you know to be successful, as your ideal. Make a practice daily of spending a few quiet moments in study of your ideal's methods and character. The person selected should be, which some call a "'top-notcher' **OR** 'a person of top-rate'," in your own line of endeavor, so that in striving to unlock the "secret door of success" they seem to have opened, you will be getting acquainted with the path which they have already traveled. If feasible to do so, become personally acquainted with your ideal. Ask your ideal's advice, or at least learn all you can through conversations with those who know them; through books they read; through things that interest them; and by all available methods — how and why they are successful.

Your ideal may, on close scrutiny, (probably will) prove "to have feet of clay" — defects of character and method. No one ever entirely meets the requirements of "hero worship." In such case, keep seeking for your ideal. But you will find by thereby personifying your ideals of business, that your Ambition is constantly fed with proper food. There is perhaps, no "perfect business person" in the world. Your ideal, of course, is your own conception of what is perfect. Select as your business model the one who seems outwardly at least, to meet your ideal. You will learn, even from their defects — and profit by them.

15

LESSON XI

ACHIEVEMENT

Achievement of Purpose marks the temporary satisfaction of Ambition and is the best proof of Success.

Other and greater purposes, and other and higher ambitions will succeed those which have been achieved, but with achievement we always feel, and therefore **KNOW**, we have been successful.

People sometimes consider themselves successful because they have achieved their own purpose in life, when their friends, unaware of the purposes or the driving power of the ambition that makes them go forward to the goal, consider them highly unsuccessful. Achievement has no value in these cases, save to the person who achieved it.

But in business, achievement that spells success to all who care to see, means arrival at the goal of financial independence, which is the immediate purpose and the primary ambition of most people who engage in business. If financial independence is not your immediate purpose; if it does not constitute your primary ambition, then you may as well avoid the business world and be content to be a financial dependent.

WHO SHOULD AVOID BUSINESS

If you are not sufficiently attracted by the Purpose of being a success in business to have any Ambition in that direction, then it is better to let business alone. Your viewpoint and that of "business people" are so different, that it is perfectly natural for them to consider you a "failure" in

99

business, where you regard yourself as a "success" — in some other line of activity.

Hence, you may utterly ignore business and business methods — but you must not complain when business people hesitate or refuse to have business dealings with you, save on a strictly cash basis — Service for Service.

You are not justified in assuming an Attitude of injured pride, or contempt for the world's business, nor is it wise, for your own sake, to assume such an Attitude, since you injure your own character by introducing this destructive element of injured pride. It may affect your whole life work in other directions than "business." Your mind becomes "biased" and cannot think in a "straight line."

Business is obviously a necessity and an essential part of the world's progress. Since we cannot do without it and continue to live in harmony with everyone around us, there is only one possible escape from contact with it.

That is, to become a hermit; withdraw entirely from the rest of humanity and produce everything we eat or wear or utilize for our own comfort or enjoyment. This is your privilege if you are attracted toward that sort of life and have no wish to remain a part of the human family — no desire to engage in reciprocal service.

ACHIEVEMENT GIVES US SATISFACTION WHEN THE ELEMENTS THAT HAVE GONE INTO IT ARE DIRECTED TOWARD SATISFACTION.

The importance of this statement lies in this:

- Ambition is the driving power of Achievement.

- Purpose is the goal of Ambition.

- Initiative provides us with Purpose.

- Memory pours out its treasures to provide us with Initiative.

- Emotion causes Memory to function.

- Vision is the seer of Truth, because it sees the natural, harmonic relations between emotions.

- Silence is the developer of Vision.

- Energy is conserved by Silence.

- Attitude directs Energy.

- Attention determines Attitude.

ATTENTION THE STARTING POINT

Only the most elementary knowledge of logic then, is required to make it apparent that Achievement of Business Success primarily rests upon the Attention you give business. It is also obvious that your Attitude must be a correct business Attitude, otherwise all the Energy you put into your work may be expended in the wrong direction.

These simple rules, each one resting upon the foundation of the one below it, and the whole being but an elucidation of the law of Self-Control, which is the master key to Success in business, would appear so simple that a child could follow them.

But human experience for thousands and tens of thousands of years has demonstrated that possibly not more than five per cent of the world's population are successful business people and women or ever have been such. This can only mean therefore, that the laws of business have been understood either intuitively or self-consciously by this percentage, or that about 95 per cent of the people in the world have always been, as they are now, ignorant or lazy.

LAZY OR IGNORANT?

That a great many people, perhaps the great majority, do prefer to have others do their thinking for them; do prefer subjection to personal responsibility; do prefer a set wage and a definite number of working hours to using their own efforts for running a business of their own — is unquestionably true. But it seems to be true also, that even this great majority adopts this attitude through ignorance, because so many of them have become inquiring critics of those who are successful in business; demanding of them impossible things; besmirching their motives and methods, whether right or wrong; decrying "business" of all kinds as "crooked" — whether it is or not.

This may not indicate laziness at all. It is certainly the result of ignorance.

In some personal researches, the writer has become convinced there are plenty of both lazy and ignorant people in the world. Laziness which the author makes no attempt to cure. But ignorance imposes an obligation upon those who **KNOW** to relieve it, just as hunger and thirst impose obligation upon those who have food or drink to relieve them.

Moreover **IGNORANCE IS AT THE BOTTOM OF LAZINESS.**

LAZINESS IS THE BREEDER OF CRIME.

CRIME IS THE DESTROYER OF BUSINESS.

BUSINESS, THEREFORE, OWES IT TO ITSELF TO RELIEVE IGNORANCE.

Achievement of success, as any successful business person can tell you, comes only after a thorough business education. No one succeeds until they have mastered the principles of success in their line of work.

These principles, set down here in a formula as simple as the writer knows how to make it, should be open to all people. There would be less trouble between "Labor and Capital" were both properly educated in the principles of business success.

DANGERS OF TOO MUCH ACHIEVEMENT

Achievement does not eternally satisfy any more than a single meal will eternally satisfy the stomach. Achievement is mental food. Our mind hunger is fed on Achievement — and we call that hunger Ambition in the business world. The business mind digests and assimilates Achievement in order to grow greater. And the greater we grow, the more Achievement the mind requires for satisfaction.

We may become mental gluttons in this way just as we may become physical gluttons by refusing to control hunger — or rather by refusing to recognize when real hunger ceases and a mere Appetite dominates.

We waste time and energy and attention in gratifying sensuous appetites. So, Achievement is a thing also to be controlled, like all the elements of success.

Achievement may become so comparatively easy to the educated person, as to be almost a matter of routine. It is at this point that so many successful business people begin their failure.

There is something in the very nature of success that lures people to their own destruction. Some, in particular, seem to demand a fight with or without provocation. Therefore many businessmen look upon business as a battle or a series of battles, which, as heretofore pointed out, is the wrong Attitude, because it is untrue. Business is the exchange of Service for Service.

Achievement travels a spiral path — always onward and upward. Each turn of the spiral goes over the same ground, but on a higher plane.

When you have succeeded in your first Ambition and achieved your first purpose, there is yet another Ambition, another Purpose to be Achieved. And when you have reached those, yet others present themselves.

There is no end to the spiral. You have only to keep your Attitude in the same direction and attend to business. You cannot slip backward.

Nature's methods and unchangeable. Deviation from them means inefficiency and failure in the exact degree of the deviation. Therefore, if your Attitude is one degree off "North" of success, you will achieve your Ambition just one degree "off."

If you punch holes in your piping of Silence through which the stream of your Energy flows, you cannot expect it to do 100 per cent work because power leaks out of every hole. Vision will be impaired to the extent Emotion is permitted to run riot and Memory is cluttered up with rubbish.

To Achieve success 100 per cent, you must yourself be 100 per cent efficient. You must have 100 per cent control of the force within you.

SELF-CONTROL DETERMINES THE MEASURE OF ACHIEVEMENT.

PRACTICE THE FOLLOWING EXERCISE DAILY

Achievement — Select daily some part of your work that you purpose to do, as just advised, then do it, if possible, more thoroughly than anything else. Devote your whole energy and attention to doing that thing thoroughly. You are, therefore, successful in that one thing. The emotion that success arouses is a power and will stimulate you to still further achievement, which is, of course, "Ambition."

Achievement, Purpose, Ambition, Initiative are four things that are complementary to each other. They make for Mastery. They require active use of all your latent powers, faculties and capacities.

16

LESSON XII

MASTERY

There is a natural business principle that impels every self-controlled individual to seek association with those things and persons like themselves but complementary to their own faculties, capacities and powers.

Note, that we do not say "Successful" individuals, but "Self-controlled" individuals. Success follows Self-control as the moon follows the sun.

Attention attracts Attention.

Whatever your Attitude, you will attract by it a like Attitude in others.

Your energy and the way you expend it, will attract like energies and methods to your own, but complementary to them.

Your Vision will attract others with like Vision.

To your Emotion, like Emotion will respond.

Memory attracts its like — which, by the way, is the secret of thought transference that all of us encounter in some form, even when we are not self-conscious about it.

Your Initiative will arouse like Initiative in others that will supplement your own, because it is a complementary Initiative.

Your Purpose will attract others with Purpose.

Achievement on your part will attract Achievement in others to aid you.

Mastery of yourself will fit you for Mastery of others and of conditions.

These statements are but simple truths that have been recognized by the most successful people in business in all ages.

Business success is not different from success of any other kind. It is governed by Natural Law.

Humanity has attempted to imitate Natural Law in their human codes regulating the social relations as Blackstone wisely observed. People's mistakes and not Nature's, are the obstacles to business success under humanity's made laws.

But the higher law always dominates the lower, so that the business person who obeys the Natural Law, need not violate the human — but control it.

BUSINESS MASTERS KNOW THEMSELVES

People who have learned the lessons of Self-control, occupy natural positions of responsibility in the business world in keeping with their Mastership, which cannot be affected by any artificial or temporary conditions whatsoever.

These individuals **KNOW THEMSELVES** and their own capacities and powers so thoroughly, that no matter what their employment may be, whether they, for the time, are ribbon clerks or factory heads. They have no fear of failure, business or otherwise.

Panics, loss of jobs, profiteering and high prices have no dominion over them. They refuse to fall into the common hysteria over such things, even when poverty closes around them and takes all their savings. For they **KNOW** the natural law will take them out of poverty again as surely as rivers flow toward the sea.

The Self-controlled individual, who knows the law and applies it, this is the "big person" as defined in the works on the dynamics of business and business people, the "big person" is the one who always comes to the top in adversity because the laws of Nature have so provided.

One authoritative source illustrated the law in a delightfully novel way. The proponent half filled a large glass globe with beans and English walnuts, mixing them thoroughly. Some of the big nuts were on the bottom, and some of the little beans were on top. But a thorough shaking brought all the big nuts on top and put the little beans on the bottom.

Being a reporter by trade, the proponent then proceeded to interview the "little beans" — (the "big Nuts" kept Silent) — and obtain their notions of why this natural phenomenon could be.

Little Bean pitied himself, and envied the big Nut. It was just little Bean's bad luck that put him on the bottom. Give him but a chance to show what he could do and he was the equal of any big Nut that ever was. So the proponent, as the god of the machine, put little Bean on top and big Nut on the bottom and once more shook them up. Little Bean went down and big Nut came up.

According to the proponent, little Bean never was able to understand and perhaps never will be, until he grows as big as big Nut. Then he won't talk about it, perhaps.

The big Nuts of this world, both good and bad, are at the top of things because they are Big. They couldn't keep themselves down in the world's shake-ups, even if they tried, without breaking themselves to small pieces and becoming as small as the little Beans.

It is pure ignorance of the Natural Law that keeps the business world in a constant Industrial Riot. The Ignorance is not, by any means, on the side of the little Beans of Labor. The big Nuts of Capital, despite their comparative size which keeps them on top, are yet not Big enough to see how much to their own advantage it would be to educate the little Beans so they, too, could know how to grow big.

And the bigger the little Bean grew, the bigger the big Nut would grow. The bigger Business there would be. The Beans and Nuts are partners.

MASTERS in business are first of all Masters of themselves. Otherwise, they soon go down before others bigger than them. Business can be only what those engaged in it make it. It undergoes inflation and contraction just as the cells of the human body are inflated or contracted by what they are fed, because the individuals who carry on Business become inflated or contracted by what they put into the body of Business.

To illustrate: Business sometimes goes reeling drunkenly around because it is intoxicated with success. And there comes the inevitable reaction — "readjustment," it is called in business life.

When an individual drinks whiskey enough to get drunk, we know that the alcohol has a certain peculiar effect upon the cells of their body, especially the nerves.

Alcohol causes the little cells to swell out and enlarge. This causes the tiny particles of solid matter in the cell, upon which the vital, positive energy is carried, to fly farther apart. The positive energy is scattered, and the cell becomes dominantly "negative." Emotions are stirred up and mental pictures of all sorts formed in a chaos of Imagination. The person is given a sense of freedom from all natural limitations. Their ego as well as their cells become expanded and for a time they imagine themselves a most wonderful Master of all they survey. Then the reaction comes — the alcoholic conditions lose their effect, contraction of the cells and the ego sets in and nausea and a headache of the "morning after" arrive. Long habit of "going on a spree" distorts the very shape of the cells and warps the whole person both physically and mentally.

So it is with the periodical "drunks" of business. Sometimes the big people of business lose their self-control and indulge in a business drunk of profiteering. But the inevitable readjustment comes as it must always come. Humanity made laws may not be powerful enough to put these dangerous people where they belong, but the Natural Law always gets them. They must pay and do pay Nature even when they seem to "flourish like a green bay tree," to those that have suffered from their depredations.

Bigger people always come to take the place of these warped and twisted and self-belittled false Masters of Business. When human criticism cannot reach them, Nature does — and administers the penalty.

The Law of Compensation invariably adjusts business disturbances as it does everything else. If you don't believe this, you had better study Business progress for the past ten years — or any other period of the world's history you choose.

Mastery comes to the one who aligns themselves with the Natural Law of Business which provides that permanent success comes only to those who give service for service.

17

A CONCLUDING THOUGHT FOR DAILY PRACTICE

MASTERY – THE REALIZATION OF SELF

This book has been in the writing, an earnest endeavor to present in simple language, the fundamentals of Business Success as they exist in Natural Law.

In order to ascertain just how effectively this had been done, the author has from time to time submitted the text to business people and women, some of them "successful" and some of them "unsuccessful" in their professions. In every instance the text has been approved, sometimes with helpful suggestions as to its betterment, by those who were successful.

Those who were not successful in their business, have invariably reported that "it helped me." Some of them, after several months have passed, write to say that by application of the information given them, they are now on the highroad to success and have either gotten or are in the way of getting what they most want in the way of business.

One very amazing result has come from the author's submission of the manuscript to friends engaged in business — a result not entirely expected. This has been a distinct tendency toward what may be called a "religious" viewpoint in business. And not at all a sectarian or denominational viewpoint, for both Christian and Jew and so-called Agnostic, have agreed that a "religious" foundation is essential to the business stability of any nation.

The author has, throughout this work, spoken of the "Laws of Nature"

108

and of "Natural forces." He is personally unable to conceive of any "Supernatural" laws or forces — for whatever is, must be "Natural."

But the age old question arises — "What is behind Nature?"

To this, many will answer — **GOD** or the Divine or the Universal Source.

But is not **GOD** or the Divine or the Universal Source, "Natural"?

Whatever one's belief may be (and we know that people worldwide, have achieved business success) it is at least an interesting viewpoint that sees **"GOD"** in Nature as well as "behind" Nature; and seeing **GOD's** omnipresence in Nature of which every human being is a part, to see divinity in **OURSELVES!**

Mysticism has perhaps never been understood by any save those who have experienced it. Perhaps it never will be. There seems to be no adequate language in any human tongue, that enables the mystic to converse intelligently with the matter of fact business person so that the business person can grasp what the Mystic is "driving at."

Yet sometimes the deepest "religious" experience comes to the business person and they "see" the very elements of business success of which this volume treats, and which they have used themselves intuitively, without being able to formulate their principles in words perhaps, in an entirely "new light."

With one such expression of this enlarged vision of Self-mastery, these lessons will be brought to a close. It was written by one whose business is to come daily in contact with people injured in mind or body and bring them back to health. This is the thought:

"I am the center of the Universe. I am the composite of all things. I am divinity's own representative. I have the potentialities, the finite and infinite qualities of the universe. I have, reposed in all that is, the spark of the Divine, which comes as a blessed gift from the eternal source. I am a Child of the Divine.

"As such, all things come from within me. All strength emanates from me. All other life revolves about me, and I am — always and ever — the Generator of Power which dominates and controls all the conditions surrounding me.

"As the child of the divine, holding latent within me the spark of its divinity, it is my duty to realize my faculties, powers and potentialities and to make proper use of them in this life. The child must be worthy of their blessings. I can only be worthy of mine by applying them to my daily life, and rightly using all the gifts and benefits which have been stored up within me.

"I must learn to control the conditions about me, regardless of what they may be. The Power is within me — it is lying dormant, awaiting right use. No one can apply it but myself, for it is under the domination and control of my own Will. Nothing is beyond me. All circumstances, conditions and happenings are but passing phases and experience of my greater life to be. The incidents of today are minute experiences when viewed from the standpoint of my greater life.

"As I grow from day to day in the expression of these latent powers, faculties and blessings centered within me, gradually my self-respect, self-reliance and self-confidence develop and establish themselves. I come to a just realization of my power and my strength; and as this self-respect, self-reliance and self-confidence develop and expand, they manifest outwardly and immediately make their impression on the outside world, revolving about me as the center. Inevitably and involuntarily the world feels this just self-assertion and responds to it, with respect, courtesy and appreciation.

"It naturally follows — as the night the day — that when an individual justly respects and appreciates their own powers and abilities, likewise will they be respected and appreciated by their compatriots, and deference will be paid to this person by those around them. It is a natural law of Life.

"As I travel my daily road of Progression, I must strive more and more to realize, respect, and appreciate the latent powers and potentialities concentrated in me. Then, and only then, can I truly and sincerely and consistently command the respect, deference, and appreciation of my fellow-beings as I pass this way along my journey of life."

THE END

ABOUT THE AUTHORS

Jorge Ramirez has made his career over several decades as a business entrepreneur. He has been very successful and has chosen to mentor others in the path to success and independence. In that time he has used his spare time in sharing information of use to the reading public at large as well in assisting others in the ways of business towards achieving self-sufficiency.

J. Norwood had a lifetime of wonderful successes, as both an independent entrepreneur and self-made businessman. In his spare time he enjoyed writing and placed his knowledge, acumen, and experience into many manuscripts and instructional pamphlets.